To my lovely wife A

Thankyou for putting up with me all these years.

I don't know where I would be today without you.

To all who wish to serve in the military.

Good on ya. The world needs men and women like you to rescue people from the Baddies.

But before you enlist, I would like you to know what you are in for.

And to all who never came back.

THE DRUM

I hate that drum's discordant sound,
Parading round, and round, and round:
To thoughtless youth it pleasure yields,
And lures from cities and from fields,
To sell their liberty for charms
Of tawdry lace and glitt'ring arms;
And when Ambition's voice commands,
To fight and fall in foreign lands.

I hate that drum's discordant sound,
Parading round, and round, and round:
To me it talks of ravaged plains,
And burning towns and ruin'd swains,
And mangled limbs, and dying groans,
And widow's tears, and orphans moans,
And all that Misery's hand bestows,
To fill a catalogue of woes.

John Scott, 1793

PROLOGUE

I'm in an old church, during the Christmas midnight mass. My wife and I are visiting her parents for the first Christmas as a newly married couple. Our wedding had been the previous summer. We had moved into our first small house after a Moroccan honeymoon, and we're still very loved up. The inside of the church is dimly lit and filled with candles, it's the same church we had been married in the previous summer. The priest is conducting the service, and we've already stood up to sing a few carols from the handed-out song sheets.

Nothing in particular triggered it off. I had been standing there with those things far from my mind when for no reason, the images came flooding into my vision. As much as I try, I can't turn it off. It's not possible to think of anything else, and I'm aware that I've started quivering all over while at the same time an acute sense of nausea sweeps over me. I'm hot, sweating, and embarrassed. Are people looking? I'm trying to concentrate on the words to one hymn we're singing, but all I can see is the blood spurting out of an enormous hole in someone's buttock. In fact, the whole butt cheek is gone, exposing the top of the femur and the socket where it joins the hip. I sit back down on the pew, eyes closed, breathing heavily. It's not going away.

"Babe, are you alright?" asks my wife. She's sat down too, leaning over to see my face. "You're white!"

"What?" I ask, trying not to draw attention to myself.

"Your face is all white" she half whispers "and you're all sweaty. Are you feeling okay?"

"I feel sick" is all I can say "….go outside".

My wife helps me out of the row of seats to the central aisle where we make our way to the back, trying to open the huge wooden doors quietly.

Outside, I did what I had become desperate to do. I took off all my layers and stripped right down to the waist, and lay down topless on the icy grass. The temperature that night must have been freezing, but it felt wonderful. I don't know how long I lay there among the gravestones, looking up at the night sky. Anna sat with me, holding my hand. She must have asked what had happened and guessed it was to do with Afghanistan, but I can't remember what I told her. Eventually I stopped quivering and started shivering with cold, so I got dressed again, cracking jokes with my wife about being half naked among tombstones on a wintry night, and now having a wet bum. Then we listened at the door and found they had stopped singing, so we decided to wait for the next song because there was no way we'd go in without a distraction. So, we stood there outside; whispering, making each other laugh until the next song came along.

It was the first time I knew something was wrong. It was totally unexpected, and very real. In later years, Afghanistan seemed to be all I could think about. I was a labourer on a building site – one of a string of jobs I worked in after I left the army – and for weeks my only real job was to clean up after tradesmen with my plastic tub and broom and throw them in the skip. Minimum wage. Later, I could be trusted with knocking up cement and loading out for the brickies. And most times during those days, I'd be thinking about war. I'd hear the radio chatter and the thwump-thwump thwump of a Chinook as it comes to get the wounded back to Bastion, and the snap-crackle-pop sound of gunfire. Visions of helmeted figures moving quietly through irrigation canals, illuminated by moonlight. I'd climb up a scaffold ladder with a stack of twelve bricks on my shoulder, playing the what-if game. What if we had used the proven route? What if I'd paid more attention? What if I'd paid less attention? What if I'd gotten a tourniquet on faster? What if I had never gone there at all but went to college and learnt how to lay bricks instead.
Some of the tradesmen get angry with me for being in a world of my own, and I want to blow their head off. But I say nothing. Sometimes I drive home from work with the noise of bullets snapping past my ears and I have to pull over and sit alone in the car with the engine off. I begin crying silently and say nothing about it. Sometimes Anna would ask questions about my tour. She knows I don't look her in the eyes when it comes to this subject and that I become evasive. She says I guard it with fists clenched tight and won't let anyone in.

I never thought that this would happen to me.

1
The Training

I came to the UK to join the army. It was the only reason why I ever came to the nation my family was supposed to be from. I googled the nearest recruiting office as soon as I unpacked my bags at the house share in Mitcham, then asked one of the many half-drunk, half-stoned South African room-mates which bus to get.
I passed all the initial interviews and fitness tests, and the recruiting sergeant talked me out of joining the infantry and instead join the Royal Engineers. I am told I can walk into virtually any career after I leave the military as a Royal Engineer, and I believe it all.

I had to wait four months until the next recruit intake begins in an Army Training Regiment in Staffordshire. On our first day of basic training, myself and other recruits are picked up by one of our training instructors at the train station and driven to the barracks. Whittington Barracks. A grey, bleak place with its parade square, armoury, its low-lying cookhouse against an overcast sky in the fading February light. The usual MOD buildings, entirely of brick with white window frames, with the smell which I would come to always associate with barrack life – deodorant and shower gel.
A lot of basic training is spent being cold and wet outside and constantly cleaning everything inside, learning how to be British soldiers. There are about forty or fifty teenagers in the training troop, including one from Northern Ireland, two Scots, one Scouser, one Welshman, four South Africans and myself: Botswana. Neither I nor the South Africans could understand the Irishman.
The troops had four sections of about eight or nine recruits and a training NCO, a corporal (full screw), is assigned to each section as their personal mentor. There is a troop sergeant in charge of the full screws and an officer who deals with the overall admin and also teaches lessons. My section's full screw was thorough with us. When he introduced himself to us, he explained how he had been frustrated in his regiment when new recruits would arrive from training with poor standards, and so had volunteered to be an instructor at an

ATR. In time, we all learned to fear this corporal and were the most obedient to him. By the end of our training, some of us began to admire him.

Mornings begin with water parade. Everyone lines up down a corridor with the issued plastic mug full of water held out in front of them. One of the full-screws walks down the line, checking the pint is full, and orders us to drink. We down the pint, and hold the mug upside down over our heads. In this way, the Army knows we have been hydrated.
"Right, three ranks, outside!" the full-screw yells.
We parade outside the block, in three long ranks stretching out into the darkness, right turn and march off in the snow toward the cookhouse for scoff.
The days are divided into lessons. We are taught drill, and first aid. We spend our first night out in the adjacent woods in six inches of snow. We are issued with weapons and given lessons on how to use them, how to strip and clean them, and how to shoot them. I had never fired a round in my life, and listen exactly to what I am taught. Every day we spend in the gym, where the PTI's get us fitter and stronger. The first thing everyone realises is that they are not as tough as they think they are. We learn a new slang word – "beasted". To get beasted is to be driven to absolute physical exhaustion as a form of punishment. To TAB is to Tactical Advance to Battle, or a loaded march with a Bergan. And a Bergen is a huge rucksack. Our first tab was only three miles, with our bergens loaded with our sleeping bags, but we all struggled to keep such a fast walking pace without breaking into a run. When they shout from the front "Double!", the whole troop breaks into a run, relieving the burning shins from having to walk so fast. We run until the instructors shout out "Quick march!", and the column resumes the fast-paced walk. "Close up those gaps!"
In time, the tabs became longer and heavier, lasting for the standard two-hour period a soldier should be able to carry his bergen with ease. Engineers needed to carry twenty-two kilos with a weapon. Infantry needed to do twenty-five. In real operations, the loads are far heavier.

When we are not outside learning field craft, or weapons handling, or in the gym getting beasted, or marching stiffly around the square, or tabbing around the local area, we are cleaning the accommodation block. We are shown how to make our beds, arrange our lockers, clean the ablutions, and buff the floor. We spend the entire evening cleaning and tidying and arranging, ironing our bedsheets and pillow cases and then sleeping on the floors. And in the morning, while still dark, we wake up and continue cleaning. Sometimes we buff the corridors all night, taking it in turns to wake up and walk the buffing machine up and down until the floor surface has a water-like reflection. Everyone takes off their boots and walks around in socks until the training instructors enter the block.

"Stand by your beds!" we hear shouting from the down the corridor. They sound angry.

Four lads in a room, stood at ease in silence, facing each other. The screws are in the first room, far away and we hear them shouting. Sometimes we stifle a laugh when we hear what is going on. The troop sergeant was shouting at the Welshman, Woody. We had just come back off an exercise the previous Friday and Woody was starting to smell. They had discovered he hadn't showered all weekend, which explained their anger. The instructors come to the next room, and this time we hear things being thrown round with the occasional comment.

A stern voice: "there's dirt still on the bottom of your trainers".

Or, sometimes an explosion of anger echoing into our room. "What's that! What the fuck is that! Have you even bothered ironing this?!" followed by the sound of metallic locker doors slamming closed. The recruit pauses, unsure of how to respond safely. "Yes Corporal". A lie. It is followed by the NCO shouting full blast at the rigid form of the stood-to-attention recruit, and the noise of objects landing on the floor. By the time the instructor reaches our room, we are all nervous. One of us shouts "Room! Room-shun!"

And in one motion we come to attention, left thigh lifted up horizontally and driven down into the floor, heels together with a force which always jars the body, back straight, arms tight up against the torso, hands in a loose fist down the thigh, pressing slightly on the thumbs. Chest out. Chin slightly elevated, staring straight ahead. Staring, yet trying to glean as much information as possible. The corporal is walking around the room. We are the fourth room he has inspected this morning, and we must be done soon if we are to get to scoff in time. He walks to my side, just within peripheral range, and I can see him standing in front of my locker. I have not touched the inside of this locker since yesterday's inspection. I have a brand-new toothbrush I have never used lying beside my un-squeezed toothpaste. He picks up my razor and closely examines the blades. It is clean because I have never used it, and as long as we are in this place, getting inspected is all that is going to happen to it. Our real toothbrushes and shaving kits are always packed away in a private draw with a padlock on it.

Room inspections only ended one of two ways. If the standard has been achieved by the time they get to your room, the atmosphere is relaxed and the training staff can even have a joke with you as they inspect the room and lockers. But if they find the troop has been lazy in preparing for the morning's inspection, it often ends with a shout for "*CORRIDOR!*" and everyone runs out and lines up down the corridor, stood to attention, staring straight ahead. There the full screws pace up and down the line, shouting, threatening, shaming and lambasting us. We are not good soldiers. We are going to get ourselves killed. We can't be asked, we are not sparking, we are not screwing the nut, we are not toeing the line, not switching on.

"Start sparking!"

"Start switching on!"

"Fucking standby!"

"Look in, gents!"

And when they're really angry with us: "On your belt buckles!" And we all quickly spread out down the corridor, and get down into the press up position, waiting. Hands shoulder width apart, beret quickly rolled and shoved into a pocket. The corporal stands in the middle of the corridor, surrounded by a sea of green Destructive Pattern Material and shiny black boots. "Down!" and everyone lowers their body down to fist height from the floor and holds it there. The training instructor is continuing his bollicking but no one is really listening, only waiting for the sudden bark "UP!" and the sea of green DPM rises again like the tide in quick motion.

"DOWN..........UP......................DOWN – a very long pause – HALF WAY UP!"

The first of the gasps can be heard from the weaker ones, trying to hold their position.

"UP................DOWN..................UP.............DOWN......
........HALF WAY UP!"
And so it goes on, the gasps and groans and determination steadily filling the room until finally he feels he has gotten his point across. "On your feet UP!" He will be making his way through the sea of people back to the troop office. "Gents, get yourselves to scoff before the cookhouse closes".

Our times off is spent confined to barracks for the first six weeks. Only after we had individually passed a drill test would be inspected and given a weekend pass, to return by Sunday night. Until then, everywhere we went to within camp had to be done marching. Recruits are not allowed to walk. Recruits had to march, swinging arms out straight in front of you, locked out at the elbows, pressing slightly on the thumb. Legs walking normally and back straight. If you were with a friend, you marched side by side, and if you were in a three, the third man went behind. Front right-hand man always called out the salutes if the group passed an officer. From the moment you left a building, night or day, you marched.
If there was one patch of holy ground on any Army camp, it is the Square. It is sacred. You must never set foot on it without highly polished boots, and never on your own. Upon this ground takes place the ancient military ceremony: drill. The priests of this ceremony are the NCO's. They love drill, they love commands, both giving commands and obeying them. In time, I would love it too.
The Square would usually have a training troop rehearsing this ceremony, with three ranks of young lads all stood to attention. "Troop will move to the left in threes........Leeeeeeeeffft *TURN!"*, followed by forty voices shouting the prescribed response "ONE! TWO-THREE, ONE!" echoing across camp as they snapped to their left. If they did it well, their boots would slam down in one unified *CRUMP*. If the troop was shoddy, forty boots would slam down slightly too early or slightly too late, making a collective machinegun fire effect.
The Square is the great tester of any troop. It is easy to see if a group of men are really a team when they are on the Square. The other great tester of underlying comradery or friction were log runs. But we did not know about those yet.

Our first drill lesson was taken by our Troop Sergeant, and the temperature must have been two or three degrees with a strong wind. We stood there at ease in three ranks, hands behind our back, trying to keep them warm but unable to move. We had been allowed to wear our smocks for this lesson, but he was dressed in only a shirt without even a t-shirt on underneath. There he stood before us with his pace stick beside him, oblivious to the wind. I thought, he has got to be cold. There's no way he isn't.

After twenty minutes, the sergeant could see we were too cold to concentrate and allowed us back to the block to get our gloves on before continuing the lesson. When it was over, when we were finally marched off the Square, back to the front of the block and fell out, everyone rushed to the radiators to try warm our hands up again. It's all conditioning. Whether it is getting used to cold environments, getting used to instant obedience, carrying heavy weight, not walking across The Square, cleaning toilets, ironing pillows, assault courses, tabbing, drill, pay parade, all those silly traditions and practises gradually turn you into someone else. We're taught first aid and map reading. We bayonet wooden dummies, screaming at the top of our lungs while the rest of the troop tries not to laugh. We shoot rifles, and run up hills and sit in the classroom listening to how important diet is. Some of us loved it, but some didn't.

After four weeks of training, recruits had the right to Discharge as of Right. We were told from the beginning that we had to serve at least twenty-eight days in a Training Regiment, and by the end of that time we would be allowed to leave if we thought we had made a mistake. About ten hands were raised and were allowed to pack their kit and go home.

After eight weeks, another one was discharged after our weekend away. We were all introduced to Compulsory Drugs Tests when we returned. We were sat in a large room, listened to the lecture on the Army's zero policy to drug abuse and then told we were not allowed to leave the room until we had individually visited the toilet, sleeves rolled up and escorted by a full screw where we were given a small test tube-like container to urinate into. It had a built-in thermometer to ensure that the urine was genuine and not swapped for any drug-free urine. That is why sleeves had to be rolled up.

One of the more promising recruits who had spent the weekend in London tested positive and was discharged. Two more were backsquadded due to injuries, which meant that they had to spend some time recovering in hospital and then joined a newer troop.

Our final exercise. It has been about fourteen weeks since Day One Week One. We are driven to Brecon and play war for a week. There is a made-up invasion by a local made-up insurgent group which we have to defeat using all our new skills as soldiers. So, we dig our shell scrapes in a wood block and set up our harbour area. From there, we begin operations. We go on section-strong patrols, sometimes setting up ambushes or sometimes walking around all night. We patrol during the day, sometimes moving to some other woods, or running an observation point overlooking a road. We lie in ambushes in the darkness watching a road and finally hear the crumple of many boots on the dirt road and the gentle bounce of webbing, and then see the dark figures illuminated by the moonlight and that final moment of tension, waiting for the machine gunners to open up so that everyone else could open up too. The adrenaline and excitement in that moment immediately expels all the cold and wet and discomfort of lying down in dew sodden grass for two hours. Sometimes at night we are attacked by enemy forces where we fire back and bug out – pack up fast and run to a prearranged rendezvous point where theoretically we would escape the ensuing mortar barrage or follow up attack.
Everyone fantasises that it is real. My childhood was spent kindling the ambition to go to war. I wanted to be in combat. I wanted get shot at and shoot back. I wanted to experience all my favourite war scenes and one day have a few of my own war stories to tell.
It would later take about ten years before I would freely say anything, and that the experiences we all craved in a comparatively short time would affect me long after I had left the army.
But I didn't know that yet.

Prior to our final exercise, we were loaded onto a coach and driven to Belgium to visit battlefield sites from the First World War. We were given a guided tour of trench systems and important hills which were still covered with grassed-over shell craters, making the landscape look more like the waves of the sea. We paraded under Menin Gate, stood to attention during the evening ceremony, underneath all the names of the missing. From where I was standing, as high as I could see without raising my head, the walls were covered with small columns of names of soldiers who had never been found.

The end of basic training is marked with a pass out parade, and is attended by families. We had been rehearsing for a few weeks now, with rifle drill. On the day, bayonets are issued out as we are waiting out of sight to march onto the square. To my right, Symms has just discovered how sharp they were by stabbing himself in the fore arm with the tip of his. He turns to the guy next to him and asks "does this look serious?" before staggering forward. His weapon is quickly taken off him while someone gets the medic.
During the parade, special prizes are given to recruits who had excelled in a certain field. Best at Drill. Best at Fitness. Best All-Round Recruit. I was awarded the Best Shot. Like everyone else, I was full of confidence and thought of myself as a fully trained soldier after only three months. We had all posed for pictures, holding our rifles and posting them onto our Facebook accounts. We were strong, fit and had been told repeatedly that we had joined the most professional army in the world. We looked the part and now looked down on 'civilian weakness'.
In reality, we knew virtually nothing about real army life or soldiering.

The Combat Engineer course which follows is hard. They sent us to Gibraltar Barracks in Surrey. We are no longer molly-cuddled as our bodies physically transitioned to civilian strength to a military standard, and our new instructors at Gib knew it. They were all Engineer corporals. You need to pass this course to be allowed into the Corps of Royal Engineers, they told us. To earn your stable belt and Engineer flashes to pin on your arm. They told us that if they were to train us by the book, we would not be nearly as fit or strong as we should be, but that they were going to do things their way. The course lasts eight weeks. A lot of the training is running, tabbing, more running, log runs, stretcher races, and endless scrapping within the training troop. When we are not fighting and running and cleaning, we are learning about combat engineering. Minefields, bridging, blowing things up and filming the explosions on our phones.

It's fun. To demonstrate how dangerous a detonator is, our training NCOs get a pig's head from the butcher, and wedge the cigarette-like silver object into its mouth. Then, for good measure we cram as much det cord as we can, light the fuse and run for cover. The pig's head explodes, scattering itself in all directions. Later, one of us finds the pig's snout. He says he'll bite a piece off and eat it if we all pay a pound each. We eagerly agree and watch him with morbid fascination as he psyches himself and rips into it, trying to tear a piece off. He finally manages to swallow some, but it's vomited up almost immediately.

The training NCOs have trouble with our troop of fifty hot headed youths, with only a few older recruits sensibly keeping out of the power struggles. They have had a good reputation until our intake came along. We seemed to do nothing right, and they didn't like our attitude.
So, they discipline us. Sometimes their punishments are noticed by senior officers and they themselves are punished for being too harsh. This makes them angrier, and so when we are away on tabs or runs, they stop us in the middle of nowhere, far from help, and punish us some more. A lot of the punishments consist of running up and down the same hill carrying ridiculous amounts of weight, with the first three men back not having to do it again. Faster and faster, and then slower and slower.
It is physically draining. One morning I wake up slightly earlier than the other three in my room and go to the ablutions. I had forgotten my wash-shave kit, so I go back to my locker. It isn't there. I look all over, but can't see it. I begin waking up the other three, thinking that someone was pulling a joke and making everybody angry at me until I realise that I had been holding it in my hand the entire time. Exhaustion can have that effect on you.

Our final exercise at Gib was four nights in the field. It was a sleep deprivation exercise, with a series of engineering tasks spread out over a wide area. We spent the first night digging our four-man trenches, finally completing them at dawn. Then we would tab to another location where a stack of heavy bridging components would be waiting for us to assemble. We would then walk for a few hours to another grid reference to assemble a water storage point.

Sometimes we would get attacked and we would throw down whatever tools we were holding and grab weapons and fight back. By the time we came to our third night, even the stronger lads were dropping on the spot to sleep on the ground for a few minutes. We were rigging a bridge for demolition, and it took the troop all night to complete. The following night was spent crawling through a minefield and marking the safe lanes.

Exercises in the army always end with a dramatic climax. Usually, it's a final attack or a final run back to camp, and it's meant to be hard. After the NCO's began firing at us in the minefield, we bugged out. Each section had taken a casualty who had to be carried to safety, and after this, the long run back to camp. The route is divided into sections and each section has a nasty surprise. Some of these surprises were 'equipment' – tires and ammo tins filled with gravel. Other parts of the route were log runs. These logs were about the diameter of a telephone pole, and were long enough for three men to run on each side, holding the rope handles. Six men on, accompanied by six more running alongside, ready to take over once "Change!" had been shouted.

The rest is hazy in my memory. We would have had to get through these obstacles, and the final assault course where Rat-Boy broke his nose diving into a puddle. We would have paraded immediately, all hot and soaking wet, filthy and muddy. Some high-ranking Engineer officer made his way down the three ranks, giving each recruit the red and navy-blue stable belt. "Welcome to the Corps" he says to me.

In four days, we had about four hours of sleep.

The training is not unlike anyone else who has passed out of Gib Barracks. At the end of six months, we are given the regiments we are posted to. Those sent to Northern Ireland stare in disbelief at what they've just been told. Everyone wants to go to regiments that are soon to deploy to Afghan. The unit I was initially posted to was going to deploy there in a few months. The handful of us were exhilarated and were the envy of everyone. I remember posting on Facebook "going to Afghanistan…yeah baby yeah!" Later on, my posting changed and one of my friends went on to the war before me. He told me on Facebook how he had been caught in a field while driving a digger, taking rounds and lying behind cover while trying to shoot back. He said his fingers were trembling when he tried to change magazines. I was green with envy. I couldn't wait. We were very fit and strong. We had all taken over a minute off our mile and a half runs and most of us could run it in under nine minutes and now we're doing guard with live ammo. We think we're hard core for passing the B3, extra tough for enduring the extra treatment. But it's the same in all armies. Everyone thinks they are tough before they join the army, and everyone thinks they are tough before they go to their unit.

2
The Unit

I'm squatting in the back of a four-tonne truck with a twenty pence coin. The temperature must have been below freezing because some of the puddles have iced over, and I can barely feel my fingers. I'm feeling very sorry for myself. With the coin I'm trying to scrape white paint off the truck. White paint is everywhere. It's run across the wooden floor boards, dripped through holes in the side of the truck and onto the wheel. Once on the tyre it had rolled onto the road, leaving a white patch of paint every couple of metres as the tyre had rotated. Earlier on, a mechanic and I had tried getting the cold engine to turn over. When we finally started it, we decided to go for a test run with it, to keep the engine going for a while. As we went off road we got stuck in thick sand, and the vehicle lurched from side to side trying to get out. Unknown to us, someone had put cans of white paint in the back, and one of them had been thrown around and was now leaking all over the back, onto the road. When we returned, our section commander came striding up to us as though he was about to knock us out. We stand to attention, confused, terrified. Then he starts yelling. He's yells and yells, and we're trying to work out what we had done wrong, until I hear the word "paint". I dare to catch a glance at the truck, at all the paint dripping down the side like entrails and I realise how screwed I am. We are both scared of this man.
"You must have been fucking ragging it!" he kept shouting, standing toe to toe with us. Neither of us can think clearly enough to remember the thick sand, all we can do is answer like rabbits in headlights: we're being honest, we were driving slowly.

This has been my latest mistake in my new squadron I've been posted to. We were in Liverpool on my first exercise with my new troop, and I'd been desperately trying to make myself invisible. I'd arrived at my regiment from training, a whole year spent at the Royal School of Military Engineering College, where the army had tried making me into a fitter. My troop commander tells me they don't need fitters in the regiment.

"I'm putting you down as a section sapper", he says. "You're just in time for the CO's winter challenge."
"How long is it, sir?" I ask
"Twenty-six miles, night nav. The squadron's been doing build up marches for it, so it's a bit unlucky you've missed all the prep work." He smiles. "But you'll get stuck in, won't you fella?"
The level of fitness at my new regiment was high, and initially I struggled with what was demanded. The mile and a half fitness run included a steep hill which left your legs feeling like lead when you got to the top. You are not allowed to stop. They said it added thirty seconds onto anyone's normal score. On Friday mornings we did 'green phys', which was usually heavier exercise than the usual exertions in the week. These were normally loaded marches, mostly running. In time these tabs became preferable. The sessions I came to dread were the log runs and stretcher races, which the British army is exceptionally keen on.
I had been in my unit for three months when my troop sergeant summons me to the office. He asks me if I wanted to go to Afghanistan. Immediately I say yes.
"It's a search tour", he added, but that was lost on me. I didn't know what that meant. Everyone was joining the army to go to Afghan, to experience what has been fostered by endless films and books and PlayStation games. Band of Brothers. Call of Duty: Modern Warfare.
I'm sent away from the troop to join others from other squadrons. There's about thirty of us, most of them Gurkhas. Together we are attached to another regiment that's due to deploy on tour in six months. All of us are then sent off to the National Search Centre to learn more about Search.

The first day of the Search Course was spent in the cinema room. We'd just seen an introduction video of what our tour would be about. I had been told it had to do with finding bombs, but I had somehow thought it would be relying on dogs or robots, like in the films. The video mainly consists of explosions. Iraqi explosions, Bosnian explosions, Northern Ireland truck bombs, car bombs, dustbin bombs. And the effects: armless, legless, headless, shapeless lumps of gore. Everyone is silent by the time it ended. I think, so this is Search. I immediately regretted my decision to volunteer, but of course by then it was too late.

One of the instructors stands up and starts his lesson. It's one of many lessons. For two weeks we sit in the class room learning the theory of search tactics. Different types of IEDs, chemical compositions, different ways to deploy a search team in different scenarios. After this, we practise in the field in search teams, made up of seven men. We search houses, we search vehicles, railway tracks, walls, compounds and alleyways. Sometimes we are tested on public venues, searching systematically from room to room with the instructors walking around observing us. That was one of the few times I actually found a dummy device. Myself and Gibbs were operating as a 'rummage pair', working shoulder to shoulder. One would follow another, searching a second time exactly the same thing the first had just been through, methodically going through every inch of wall, floor and ceiling. We were in the main auditorium, and checking under the stage, when I saw a small plastic lunch box among cluttered rubbish. It was filled with what looked like orange play-dough.

"Semtex" said one of the instructors, when I called 'find' and pointed it out. "Well done."

It was one of the few times I didn't get killed and step on it, or miss the device all together. I wasn't turning out to be a very good searcher, or confident at it.

I was completely surprised when I passed the course, along with the rest of our team. Of that intake, only two were deferred for retests.

By that time, I was dating a teacher living in London. Every chance I got I caught the train in from Kent to see her. It had not been long after our first date that I volunteered for Afghan. Anna didn't know too much about the war that I would be going to in a few months.

"So what exactly is going on there?" she asked one day. "Is it more like rioting and police work?"

So we type 'Afghanistan combat' on YouTube and watch some news reports. Bizarrely, I thought she would be more attracted to me for it. Instead, she hugged me and began crying. "I don't want you to go," she said.

"I don't want to go either," I admitted, surprising myself by saying it. My enthusiasm for war was deteriorating the closer we go to our deployment. We were getting briefed on the progress of the Counter IED taskforce that were already out there, whose place we would be filling when they came home. One I remember had lost three of his limbs after he made a mistake with a booby-trapped doorway. Most of his team had also been injured by the explosion. Every week there were casualties announced in the news, and some of these had a profound effect on everyone when we heard of the details.

Still, the training continued. We practised on training areas made to look like Afghanistan. Sometimes a team member in another team missed an IED and this always left a bad feeling on that team.

By now, I hated search. We used the old Grudges from the Northern Ireland days, which were long black poles which you waved at the ground in front of you like a wand. It whined whenever it passed metal. We had only been given Vallons to play around with during the Military Rehearsal Exercise, where each team had been individually assessed and authorised to deploy. There had only been five Vallons available on the temporary camp the squadron was accommodated in. We were all told to 'make sure you get your hands on one to get some experience with it, even if you have to beg borrow or steal one'. There must have been over a hundred of us. When I finally got my hands on one, I was impressed at how much better it seemed to be than the Grudge, and looked at it as my saviour. Perhaps this would make me a better searcher.

I'm sitting on the football field, relaxing. Some squaddies are playing some five aside, and others are gathering around the barbeque that is just getting lit. Earlier on we had all been told about another amputation of a searcher on tour, and its cast a tense mood on everyone which we are all trying to ignore. I got caught earlier that afternoon reading the Bible by Gibbs, who had stormed off angrily. "We're not going to die!" he said, taking it to be a bad sign. I remembered the story of King Saul, how he so desperately wanted to know whether he would be killed in the next day's battle that he went to that fortune teller. I understood exactly what he felt.

Two months to deploy. That summer, we were given a break from training and granted leave. Anna and I visited my family in Crete. Because my family live all over the world, we didn't get to see each other very often. They liked Anna, and spent all day on the beach or at the pool with her. Everyone has asked about my deployment. What will it be like? How dangerous is it? Will I be based at Bastion? I tell them all we have been told.
"I think we'll be rotating teams, some out on the ground, and then back to Bastion. So a lot of it will be spent safely at camp."
This was partly true, but it was just one of the many rumours. It was hard to know what to expect, because I had never been to war before. What I did know is that I had become very cagey about it. I did not want questions. I didn't want to explain anything to anyone, or watch the news or think about death. I wanted to do my tour, and get it over with without ever talking about I how felt. I wanted to know if I would be alive in a year. I desperately wanted to know the outcome.

Four weeks to deployment. I sweep the Vallon in front of me and take one more step. I'm the last of the four searchers, with the rest in front of me. Because we had made the mistake of getting too close to each other, the air was filled with the chatter that Vallons make when in close proximity to another. It must have been that which prevented me from hearing my own as it swept over a pressure plate. I step on it, and behind me a door chimes goes off. *Ding Dong!*
At first, I stop, confused. "What the hell was that"?
The instructor who had been silently observing us frowns, shaking

his head. He reaches down and pulls out the pad I had stepped on. The circuitry had been connected to the door chime instead of a detonator. It was my latest death. Our team leader, Smudge, has thrown his helmet on the floor and has hands in his face as he tries controlling the mixture of fury and impending doom. We are not doing well as a team, and I am sure I am the worst of the four searchers.

We had all come back from summer leave tanned and 'battle fat', the weight gained prior to a tour to compensate for all the weight soldiers lose. We go on the range, live firing. Close quarter battle, pistol shoots, advance to contact. Ambush drills, watch and shoot. We throw grenades. We fire machineguns. Firing from trenches, firing on the move, firing prone, firing from buildings, firing from vehicles. Targets that pop up suddenly, targets that move quickly from side to side. Always running on that shingle with full body armour. We also practise that all important drill, the elephant in the room: casualty evacuation.

"Stop fucking around!" they would stand over you and shout, "and get that *fucking* tourniquet on him!" "Don't just look at him, fucking pick him up! Pick him up! *Pick him up!* Your oppo's fucking bleeding to death and all you's can be fucked with is how you *fucking feel!* Now stop making those fucking girly noises and start doubling!"

They teach us that a man has four minutes to live if he has lost a leg. If both legs are lost, that time is halved. If he is lucky the explosion has cauterised the wound. Most of the injuries in Afghanistan are "catastrophic haemorrhages." Amputations from explosions. We had seen footage of traumatic wounds during our team medic course. It was an attempt to prepare us for how grotesque these injuries could be. One clip was the aftermath of a mortar bombardment in Bosnia. The cameraman had walked around with the lens pointed down at the floor, filming the bodies. We let out involuntary gasps of horror as we watched one fatal wound after another.

The second round of footage they showed us was mainly from the

Iraq war. It was to impress upon us the need to react to enemy fire before tending to the casualty. One clip showed an American soldier get hit in the head. The man next to him dove for cover, but then paused and came back where he tried dragging the body of his friend off. Another tracer round comes into the camera's view and kills the second man. In another clip, no fewer than three soldiers were killed by the same sniper because none of them did anything other than watch in shock as the man before them fell dead.
"You must win the firefight," the medic said. "I know your first reaction would be to get your mate, but this is what happens if you haven't won it."

The last night spent at our barracks. We had all been given an enormous cardboard box to pack all our belongings in our rooms. Now our rooms are empty except for this great big box. In case we are killed, our personal effects are safely sealed up in the box ready for the Quartermaster. I had had a dream the previous night. I was on the travelator at camp and I saw the flags by the NAAFI flying at half-mast. I asked a passing Gurkha what had happened, but he did not respond.
That night I got the train into London and met Anna at Waterloo. We walk around Piccadilly. Everything is hard. It's a warm Saturday night, and is filled with people having a good time. I think to myself, all these people are going to live. It's not fair that I have finally found a beautiful girl who loves me, and now I'm off to fight a war. I'm not even very good at it.
The worst part was saying goodbye. That was very, very difficult.

3
Bastion

About six months remaining

Early the next morning, around two or three o clock, we gather at the POL point and get on the waiting coach. We arrive at Brize Norton by seven and join a hundred other soldiers dressed in desert camouflage, wondering what was happening. Eventually an RAF officer announces a delay. Our flight is postponed 24 hours. He has not finished speaking before plans are being drawn up on mobile phones. My plan involves Anna, and within a few minutes we have arranged to meet up again. I catch another train into London, dressed up in desert kit and stand around Paddington Station waiting for her. A couple of times, people walk up to me and shake my hand.
"Thanks for what you're doing" they say.
Eventually Anna comes, all smiling. We hang out at the station, eat a pub dinner, and walk around arm in arm, wondering what to say, trying not to keep looking at the time. One woman walks past us and says "Cheer up love, 'e'll be alright" in a Cockney accent.
Eventually, I must leave. She stands on the platform, squeezing me and it must have been the typical scene played out in the wars: women saying goodbye to soldiers on train platforms. We wait until the automatic doors start beeping as they close, and I have to let her hand go.

At four in the morning the RAF hotel's tannoy system in each room wakes us up. Later, when everyone gathered in the lobby for the shuttle buses to the aeroplane, our Troop Commander noticed someone missing.
"Where's Smudge?" he asked, clearly agitated. The buses had been taking men to the check in counter, and we were among the last in the hotel lobby.

Smudge is nowhere to be found. Most of the soldiers had gone into nearby Oxford for a last night of heavy drinking, including most of our team. He is not answering his phone either. The last bus pulled up outside the entrance. At that moment, out of the bushes stomps Smudge. He has cuts on his hands and foliage in his hair. He reeks of alcohol, but doesn't seem drunk. Just really fed up. He has been walking for a few hours, having been stranded taxiless somewhere in Oxfordshire, trying to find which way Brize was. He said his epic journey took him across fields, through cow herds and over electric fences. Finally, in desperation he knocked on the window of a house asking for help with directions. Everyone listens, trying not to laugh because he's still angry.

Our plane landed in Germany, where we got off and were herded into a hanger for an hour to wait. Then we were herded onto an RAF Tristar to continue onto Cyprus, where we got yet another one for the final leg to Kandahar. As we made our descent, the pilot ordered everyone to put their body armour and helmet on in case of ground fire. Then the lights were dimmed. I look out the window into the night and see only darkness. I can't delay this any longer. This is actually going to happen. A few are still joking around because in reality the odds of getting hit are very small. As we made our approach, the engines suddenly rev up and the plane banks to one side. Everyone wonders what is going on, until the pilot announces the airfield was being mortared and Apache helicopters were getting priority over the airspace. As a result, he explains, they wouldn't have enough fuel to keep circling indefinitely, so they had been directed to Minadh instead. Everyone starts cheering and laughing. Minadh? Where is Minadh? I ask the man next to me.
"It's in the UAE!" he says.

We finally landed at Kandahar at night. The aircraft empties of its soldiers, climbing down the staircase, grab the piles of bags being unloaded with the rifles, and are loaded into the line of waiting local buses. No one is really talking. I haven't said a word, but just taking it all in. So this is Afghanistan.

The first thing I notice is the hot air, even at night. I gaze out of the window of the third world bus as the convoy moves slowly throughout the airport. We pass the civilian terminal, the tops of it visible above tall grey anti-blast walls. There are bored looking soldiers sitting on armoured vehicles with weathered looking machineguns with the belts of live ammo hanging out of the side. There are Alsatians, and pickup trucks, and big lorries with an array of ornaments decorating the front, and tassels hanging from the front bumper. There are signs with a picture of a camera with a red line running through it with the words "NO PHOTOGRAPHS" in a few languages. There are blue-tinged floodlights, and on the airfield there are the military helicopters. Chinooks, with the rotors all sloping downwards, and the evil looking Apaches. The inside of the bus is rocking back and forth over the dirt road, and its clammy with sweat and dust which quickly cakes the inside of your nostrils. There is a small blue fan fixed to the ceiling and it moves from left to right in lazy arcs, and the local driver is listening to Middle Eastern sounding music.

The buses take us to some tents surrounded by chest high hesco walls: sheets of metal grill forming a box, lined with hessian and filled with sand and rocks. It's a waiting area on the edge of an airfield. Inside are chairs facing a flat screen TV tuned into British Forces Broadcasting Service, an urn with coffee making kit, and a table piled with old books. The whole area of the tent is laced with more hesco to prevent everyone being killed should the tent take a direct hit.

From this tent, troops are ushered away by different RAF NCO's with clipboards reading out destinations. Besides Kandahar, there were only two others. Kabul and Helmand. Most were bound for Helmand, being loaded onto C-130s while the rest waited for their names to be called out, drifting off to sleep on wooden benches or plastic chairs.

Dawn had broken when our names were finally announced. A large group of us left the tent with all our kit, and made our way to the aircraft waiting with its engines running. We were loaded like cattle by more RAF crew, sitting along the sides of the plane against the red netting. Within a few minutes, I fell asleep, propped up on each side by the shoulders of the man next to me.

The jolt of the C-130 woke us all up. As we piled down the ramp, I caught my first glimpse of Helmand. It's very bright. The dust on the ground is like earth-brown talcum powder, and it quickly gets everywhere. In the distance are the mountains dimmed by a bright haze which still pose a threat to aircraft because of the enemy which are hiding in them. Aircraft have to land and take off very steeply, banking hard to one side to avoid flying over them.

Straight after landing at Bastion, we're loaded into the back of trucks and driven the short distance to the CIED task force lines. The camp is a collection of enormous tents erected in order, separated by a grid of well-built roads and storm ditches which were deep enough to double as slit trenches. There was a bus route with several bus stops, between Bastion 1, Bastion 2 and the American Camp Leathernecks which were all adjacent to each other.

Everywhere were tents. There were the biggest tents for the cookhouses and gyms. There were tents for each unit's ops room, surrounded by smaller tents for accommodation. Each tent had an air-conditioning unit outside, and was paved with a plastic walkway which made a *clack clack clack* sound whenever it was walked on. The CIED lines were very near the flight line, and there was the constant *thwump thwump twump* of helicopters and higher pitched *buzzzzzzz* of C-130s taking off. Some helicopters had loads underslung, some were massive Chinooks taking men to different parts of the province. Some were Apache attack helicopters with their deadly array of machineguns and rockets. Sometimes a Chinook would not fly to the flight line but would go straight overhead to the hospital helipad, sending up a giant dust cloud over the cookhouse tents. There a team would load a wounded soldier onto the waiting ambulance. I was surprised at how often this happened. There seemed to be far more casualties than was shown on the news.

Each team is quickly shown their tent where their kit will be kept throughout their tour, and then we're directed to another large tent down the road. Here we received lecture upon lecture on life in Afghanistan. Some lectures were from a Medical officer on sexual health, who handed out little metal containers containing condoms. Other lectures were about the threat of espionage inside Camp Bastion, from locals who were employed to work inside the camp. Some had been caught cutting the wires to communications antennae, and at least one sophisticated listening device had been discovered planted in the office of a senior commander. The main topic was improvised explosive devices, which by that stage of the war was the main cause of casualties. They only served to unsettle already nervous men, many of whom were on their first tour.

That night we saw mortars firing flares into the night to illuminate sections of the perimeter. A line of parachutes was drifting slowly to earth, casting long figures on the sand. There were occasional booms in the distance but no one but the new arrivals seemed to take any notice. The inexperienced soldiers shot inquisitive glances at each other but asked nothing.

Later on I bumped into a guy in my section in basic training. He had been sent to a different unit that deployed before us and was just finishing his tour. It wasn't long into the conversation before I asked him what it was like.

"Waheed's kicking off" he says and then shows me all the bruises he's got all over his legs from hitting the dirt all the time. He was tanned and looked skinny. I remembered him from training as still unsure of himself, but that seemed to have gone. Then he cocked his head to one side and says "I can't wait to get out of here".

The next day our induction to the war continued. We attended more lectures outside at the barma lanes. These were simulated stretches of roads and wadis and compounds where new arrivals were tested on their counter-IED drills. All troops had to know the basics of booby-traps. In one corrugated iron shelter, we listened to yet another lecture on what to not touch. Sticking out of the ground beside the lecturer, a grossly over-weight woman in the RLC, were various objects protruding innocently from the ground, waiting to kill us. She seemed to derive pleasure in her knowledge of these items which killed and maimed, instilling fear into her audience. To drive home her point not to touch anything, she prodded a pressure plate partially hidden in the sand. Immediately behind the hut, half a stick of plastic explosive detonated with a sudden sharp *BANG!* causing everyone to involuntarily duck in their seats. "Fucking hell" Smudge mutters next to me.

Never touch anything suspicious. Never throw away old batteries. Never walk on unsearched ground. Never set a routine. Never get channelled. Never travel in a straight line. Never trust locals. Never insult locals. Never shoot locals. Never waste your luck on silly things like cards. Never relax. Never sleep.

Each team was again individually assessed by an experienced search team that was at the end of their tour. They were tanned and their desert kit was faded. I listened to everything they had to say about IEDs, mentally willing them to say it was actually easier than it's made out to be. They didn't. Instead they went over the drills again and again. Individuals were tested on smaller lanes. Each lane was about ten metres long and had two items buried in each, and we were called up one by one and started sweeping the Vallon across. When my turn came up, I quickly got a strong hit on a patch of ground. It gave me enormous confidence. I got down prone with my feet crossed and began carefully sweeping aside the powdery soil at arm's length, coming in from one side like we had been taught. I imagine I am doing this for real, that all my searches are going to be this easy and that the reason why I had struggled through training was because they were making it exceptionally hard. When the soil falls away revealing the battery pack, I turn awkwardly to the side and shout "find!" as if I knew exactly what I was doing and wasn't at all scared of uncovering a live bomb with my fingertips.

A huge sand berm dotted with sangers divided the safe confines of the camp with the open desert. Americans manned the sentry posts, keeping an eye out as they opened the gates for us. About fifty soldiers marched in file between a couple of Mastiffs and Jackals, mounted machine guns facing outwards at the empty desert. We walked about half an hour, parallel with the perimeter of the camp, to the outside ranges which the British army used for live firing. There was a hollow square made of three earth berms, serving as the fifty-metre range. Here we were to zero our rifles again, though before that we needed to clear the range of potential IEDs that might have been buried. We were told to form an extended line, shoulder to shoulder, and walk slowly down the length of the range, carefully looking at the ground in front. If any patch of ground looked like something was buried, we were to call a man with a Vallon, and he would check it for us.

No one moved. I remember everyone looking around to see what others would do. We were actually being ordered to walk over open ground, outside camp Bastion, looking for IED's with just our eyes. Of all the stupid orders I had had to follow when I was in the army, this was by far the dumbest. Some of the senior officers, including our Troopie went off in disbelief to have a word with the officer in charge, but eventually the line of soldiers started moving forward, watching the ground. Some were joking around, shaking their heads. After all we'd been told about not getting channelled into an area, about not setting patterns, here soldiers were getting marched out of camp each day, to the same place, doing the same thing. I looked around at the camp perimeter. I couldn't see any sangers, which meant that they couldn't see inside at night.

"I can't believe we're doing this", I heard Smudge say. "This is fucked up."

Behind us, a soldier with a search dog had stayed at the start line. He had refused to send his dog down with a VO (Victim Operated IED) threat. Things might have been different had we refused as well. Later that day I walked a little way into the desert to urinate. Right beside my boot, I saw a piece of discarded wire. I stooped down and picked it up. It was a piece of twin flex. I showed it to the soldier pissing next to me, but neither of us really thought much of it. The desert is full of rubbish.

We took turns firing again into the desert, firing from fixed locations on the sand berm repelling mock Taliban attacks. The link men run up and down the thick sand with fresh magazines panting and sweating in the heat, and we reload and fire again. An empty cartridge flies out of my chamber, hits the post next to me and bounces back onto my neck, lodging itself beneath my armour. Its red hot and leaves a nasty looking scorch marking its progress down my shirt.

We wait our turn on another training serial. Teams ahead of us advanced to contact over the sand, taking it in turns to run and shoot, getting closer to the targets, and then fire and manoeuvre back again to where they started. They were staggering with exertion and dragging back a man pretending to be a casualty.

"Someone get some fucking rounds down!" one of the training staff shouts as they wandered up and down the line, and one of the machine gunners spins around and lets off a quick series of burst that goes booming down the range.

Soon it was our turn. We advanced to contact in our teams, firing and manoeuvring up to some mounds of earth, shooting at figure eleven targets. One of the mounds to my right goes up with a loud pop, and a cloud of dust flies into the air. The DS are there, shouting that there is a casualty. It's Gibbs. I ran over to him, already reaching for the tourniquet in my map pocket. I fumble around with it, and clumsily begin putting it on.

"Hold on there fella" the DS says behind me. He reaches down and puts his hands underneath the strap. It's too loose to begin twisting. "Make it tighter than that, that's far too loose."

Little Steve and I take one of Gibbs' arms and begin dragging him back. It's a hell of a long way to the start line. Everyone else is falling back, taking turns to fire and run. Steve and I must have dragged Gibbs about twenty metres when something strange happened. At first, I tripped and fell on my face beside Gibbs, the heavy ECM[1] crashing into the back of my helmet and rifle banging into my knees. I swore and got up, carried on dragging Gibbs and then before I knew it, I was on the ground again. My legs weren't working. They kept tripping into each other. What the hell's going on? I managed to slur. Someone took over dragging Gibbs. I didn't know what I was doing but was aware I was walking aimlessly in the desert and remember applying the safety catch before falling hard on the ground. I lay on my back, fumbling to get my body armour off. I couldn't do anything. A medic is standing over me, ripping off the vest and pouring water on my chest. I was vaguely aware of being helped into the shade of a Mastiff that would drive me to the field hospital, my fingers cramping up like claws.

Two days after we had finished on that range outside the wire, another group of soldiers freshly arrived in the country were marched out. As they formed an extended line to show weapons clear, one of them stood on a device. He was killed. The three men next to him were severely wounded. One of them died on the way to the hospital but the medics managed to bring him back. One of the Gurkha teams that trained with us was called out to search a safe route through for the surviving troops who had had to stay exactly where they stood until help arrived. They said later they found three more IEDs which had been buried in the area that had been frequented. The man killed had been in the country less than a week. When I heard the details, I remembered the wire I had found when pissing in the desert. That was how inexperienced and naïve I was.

---

[1] Electronic Counter Measures, designed to block any signals to a remote-controlled bomb

I spent a night in hospital and was discharged the next day. They had pumped some kind of fluid into my arm to rehydrate my body. The nurse asked me how much I had had to drink that day. It was nowhere near the daily intake of water we needed.
During the night the man across from me had a visit from a couple of officers. He was a Fijian man and had a dazed look about him and some kind of head wound. His visitors had come to congratulate him, talking about some brave thing he did.
The bed to my left was closed off with curtains. In the morning this man also had visitors, but I couldn't see who he was or what was wrong with him. Whoever he was, he was crying. I could hear sobs and sniffs. I guessed that he might have lost some limbs, and that his visitors were friends of his until he suddenly cried in a loud voice *"Allaaaaaaah!"* and broke down into sobs again. One of the English voices mentioned the prisoner with the leg wound. I looked around the hospital ward, looking like a modern hospital, wondering how much of a culture shock this must have been to the prisoner. What did the Taliban look like? I tried seeing if there was a gap in the curtains to take a look, but the guard was still there and I didn't want any more attention than what I had managed. I had been in the country for five days and already I was in hospital, sharing a ward with soldiers who had real injuries.
During my overnight stay in hospital my team was sent out on the ground without me, one man short. Their first search produced a result. One of them was searching a corner of a wall and got a very low hit which would usually be ignored. He was so scared however that he decided to check it out anyway and found wire running between his legs to a pressure plate behind him. The charge that was later blown up in situ was one of the big ones that would easily have blown to pieces the victim, as well as killing or wounding any others nearby.

4
Nadi Ali
Still about 6 months remaining

My journal shows it was still eight days before the massacre at Blue 2-5, and two weeks after I had landed in the country that I left the wire for the first time. My team had suddenly appeared back at Bastion only to be turned about and be rerouted for another area. A truck drove us there with a few other soldiers riding in the back loaded with weapons and kit. Soldiers waited around the smoking area shelter waiting to be told what to do and occasionally someone from the RAF would come and read out some names and take the men off in the direction of a certain chopper. There were a few Americans, but most were British infantry. Just after nightfall, our names were called. We joined the others and made our way to an awaiting Chinook, rotors spinning and hot air blasting out the back. We filed in and took our seats either side of the luggage. Rifle pointing downwards, like everyone else's to my left and right, and opposite. Suddenly the engines got louder and before I knew it, we were already airborne into the night sky.

I can't remember how long the flight was but it was to a place called Nad-i-Ali. The helicopter began descending and flew like a rollercoaster ride, banking left, then right, then low, then levelling off. Each time we banked left I could see out the gunner's window. The gunner was crouched over his machine gun and every now and then would lean out the window, looking down at something. Over his shoulder, I could see the terrain. It looked like square patches of fields and I caught a glimpse of a moonlit hut tinged in night-blue, surrounded by palm trees. It's gone in a flash. This is the place that I've heard so much about, where mortars and machineguns and airstrikes and IEDs and suicide bombers and kitchen knives have taken so many lives.

When a helicopter lands, everything is done fast. Before we knew it, we were right over the walls of the compound and the chopper flares, meaning the nose lifts up in the air and tail slopes down at the ground in an effort to lose speed quickly before touching down. Everyone undoes his seatbelt, grabs something from the pile of kit that sits between the two lines of soldiers, and hobbles off as best he can with helmet sliding down your head and rifle swinging from the harness on your body armour, banging against your shins. Kit is dumped, and chains are automatically formed, off-loading the Chinook usually in about a minute. There's always a line of other soldiers already there patiently waiting to depart, and they don't mind any of this last-minute work, because they're out of there. As soon as the last of the incoming kit is off loaded, the loadmaster directs the departing men to start boarding, and the entire process is repeated in reverse order. No one says anything this whole time, because the engines are never switched off, the rotors are still thumping loudly. You can't hear anything, but that's alright. Everyone just knows what to do.

When the last of the kit and men are on, the guys who just got there all crouch down away from the Chinook, looking downwards because at that moment the engines, which were loud already, just got louder. There's an enormous gust of wind which sand blasts everyone for a second, and then its suddenly quiet. I looked up at the sky just in time to see the giant Chinook, the only umbilical cord to safe, civilised Bastion, lumbering off into the night.

Shawquat seemed to be the ruins of an old fortress. The main mud walls are still standing, with the guard towers and firing holes, now all complimented with modern fortifications of Hesco. Hesco walls are like enormous sandbags, reinforced with steel wiring and higher than a man. It's very good protection.

I had heard all about FOB Shawquat back at Bastion when I was in hospital. Nurses had brought in an RLC soldier who had just been brought in by the MERT. He was a tall ashen-faced looking lad who had been burning rubbish by the burns pit when a round came in over the walls and hit him in the arm. It was from some fighting a mile away and was a complete fluke. He said it felt like a brick had fallen from the sky and hit his tricep, which immediately went numb. We had been shown our tent later that night while Troopie had gone off to get briefed about what we would be doing the next day. His return was to be the first of what was to become the normal nightly routine of fear-instilling and consequent sleep deprivation I was to get accustomed to over the months, and it always began with the map.

The team pours over the spread-out map, an aerial photograph, studying it as he is talking and pointing to various features on it. Where the Front Line of Enemy Troops are. Where are the friendlies in the area, actions to be taken if we sustain a casualty, any recent IEDs, any recent contacts, as much information as we can get. I took none of it in. That first night, a twinge of fear was snuffed out by excitement and curiosity. One phrase had kept going over and over in my mind. "Likelihood of kinetic activity tomorrow is high". One question dominated my mind. What was the fighting like?

Its early morning, and still grey. We've just clambered out of the Mastiff right outside an Afghan National Police compound. The ANP are milling about, all relaxed-looking in their grey blue uniforms, just watching us. I remember one of them was up on the roof, kneeling prostate as he did his prayers. Although I'm also trying to look as relaxed and calm as everyone else, there's really just one thing on my mind- IED's. I'm always keeping an eye at the ground, and as we're setting off walking behind another Mastiff, I quickly catch on to what the others are all doing - walking in the fresh tyre tracks. I'm already nervous but trying not to show it, fully aware that in training I had found a grand total of three IEDs without stepping on them.

We walk past locals who have come out to watch the soldiers. There are children, and it seems to relax us all. The Afghan men stare as we walk past and don't say a word. None of them showed any emotion whatsoever. It's impossible to read them. Maybe they're actually on our side but are scared to show it, because they knew something that I was still oblivious to - that the Taliban were watching everything. Gradually, the more time I spent out on the ground, the more this became plain. We were being watched the moment we left the front gate. But because this was still my first day, I'm really ignorant to that even though I'm trying my best to look the part. Maybe the locals I just passed actually do hate me. Maybe they'd watch in suspense the way football fans mentally urge the winning goal, as I wonder off towards a bit of road where they know a bomb is hidden. Calling their kids to stop playing and get indoors now. Maybe those people I smiled at would later go off, dig up their AK-47s and PKMs, meet up with their friends with RPGs and begin shooting at us when we're not expecting it. Or maybe they're just digging irrigation channels in their fields. I never could tell.

At a T-junction we passed a giant of a soldier, who had just a few days left to live, directing traffic down one turn off towards the FLET[2]. Our task, my first real search, was a culvert. I was keeping myself under control, though actually I'm very scared. This isn't practising. This is now real. Back in those days, it was still hot. Winter had not yet set in, so getting into the water of this irrigation canal wasn't so bad. I have to carefully search all around the culvert, finally getting into the water and make my way towards it to make sure there's no bomb underneath. Lee is doing the same on the other side. There's an ANA[3] detachment escorting us, together with a British mentoring team. One of the ANA soldiers is squatting just off to my left, leaning on his rifle and staring intently at the ground ahead of me.

I don't know what I'm doing.

I'm trying to remember all the things I had been taught during our six months of counter-IED training, but I'm so nervous I can't think clearly and end up brushing the same patch of ground over and over again with a gloved hand, too scared to acknowledge there was no bomb there. Too frightened to move onto the next bit of earth.

Little Steve and Gibbs have been tasked to begin searching the next stage of today's main effort - a small mud building. It had been decided by someone sitting over an aerial photograph back at Bastion that this area of Nad-i-Ali needed a check-point right there. Before our combat engineers could go to work in fortifying it, the Search Team needed to check it for booby-traps so none of them get blown up whilst working. And all the while this is going on, the

---

[2] Front Line of Enemy Troops

[3] Afghan National Army

infantry were in place in a big circular cordon, protecting us from the Taliban who we knew had been watching our efforts all morning. Towards noon, they contacted us. It starts with that crackling, popping noise with occasional whistles overhead. It sounded exactly like fireworks. It was alarmingly close and my heart immediately began beating faster. I was unsure what to do. Part of me wanted to grab my rifle and run towards it, while another part frantically searched the near ground for some cover within bolting-distance. The firing further down the road started light and sporadic but quickly got heavier, though no one could see anything or make out what was happening. The intensity came in waves, getting faster and faster, and then suddenly stops for a few seconds before starting all over again. I had just been detailed off to begin searching an area on the other side of the building when suddenly the noise of fighting erupted from the other direction, down the road we had just come from. Fear and adrenaline were pumping through my body. It was to our rear. I glanced longingly behind me where the rest of the team were. They were all searching their areas, while my search was taking me further and further away. Ahead of me, there was nothing but this empty field. I couldn't see anything beyond the trees. There could be our lads there, or there could be Taliban, so while I'm concentrating on the ground and sweeping the Vallon with my left hand, my right hand has got my rifle pointing slightly over in that direction. All it really achieved was to make me feel a little bit safer. That's when Big Steve came over to tell me the Taliban were attacking the soldiers at the T-junction we had passed down the road. He seemed pretty calm about it, as though he had just told me the football score. He tells me to finish up where I was and dress back to the building.

About five minutes later I'm walking back to him when I hear a noise like a *whoosh* pass close to my head. I don't know what it was, but in a second, I was flat on the ground in the muddy field. One of the infantry looked down at me and started laughing.

"What the hell are you doing?" he laughed.

I looked up at him. "Seriously, you didn't hear that?!" I said in disbelief. I'm getting to my feet, still half crouched, looking nervously down the road.

"Nope....hear what?"

"Something just fucking flew past us!" He looks down the road and moves closer against the wall, but still looks relatively unphased.
Back on the road, the ANA detachment was also listening to the firing, trying to work out what was going on. We had finished searching in and around the building- there just remained one small side room that had been locked. It was full of old junk but no one wanted to force it open. Not long before, a searcher had lost both his legs and an arm when he opened a door that had an IED on the other side. He was lucky to have survived. It was possibilities like these that later kept me awake each night, and it was also why we thought it safer to just blow the door off. As far as we could tell, no one was in it when we shouted out our warnings in Pashtun. Our ATO[4] set some det-cord around the door with a small charge and after we had set the film rolling on our digital cameras and balanced them on top of the wall, we all took cover after balancing our cameras on the wall to film the explosion.
"Firing! Firing NOW!" and a small boom. We peer over the wall to discover the door was still there looking untouched. So out goes Jim again, this time with a couple sticks of PE4. Cameras go back on the wall, all reset.
This time the explosion was much bigger and the cameras all flew off the wall, along with everything else. It was like the wall had shaken itself off of all the dust that was on it. Some helmets peer over to see the dust cloud settling. The door had been blown inwards, destroying the contents inside.
Attention quickly turned back to the road. That ANA detachment that had been watching our attempts to blow an old metal door off suddenly bomb-bursted in all directions, but mainly backwards, as a burst of firing came much nearer than the rest. High pitched cracks. We were scattering too, also mainly backwards, instinctively fighting each other get back round the corner of the wall. I smashed my hip doing that, though I didn't really notice at the time.
We spent the rest of the time unused and sitting behind the wall listening to the shooting down the road, eating lunch out of the ration bags and hearing occasional bullets whistling overhead.

---

[4] Ammunition Technician Officer, responsible for defusing or detonating the device once it has been found

It's much later on that day. The firing has stopped now for about an hour and locals were going about their business again. Tractors towing trailers piled sky high with the harvest go trundling by with children - who actually lived here - riding on the back waving down at us. Much later on in life, when I had my own children, I found it hard to understand how families with children could live in such an environment with explosions and gunfire every day.

The combat engineers had begun working on that building as soon as we declared it safe, and were making quick progress in fortifying it. An armoured vehicle had magically appeared as if from nowhere and delivered a load of materiel the sappers had been waiting for. Beams of wood of various shapes and sizes were placed out along the ground along with layers of Hesco material. Carpenters with rifles slung across their backs attacked the pile of wood with saws and measuring tapes, like vultures crowding around a carcass.

We had been lazing around inside, eating our lunch and getting out of the sun until it became clear we were just getting in the way, so we sat outside waiting to find out how we were getting back to FOB Shawquat. I took the time to try and chat with some of the ANA soldiers. One of them spoke very limited English, which was enough to encourage them to attempt to explain how the contact went back at the T Junction earlier when the Taliban had tried flanking us from there. The two of them were drawing maps in the dirt and placing stones - one stone for each man.

"Taliban", he said, holding up a stone, and placing it strategically along a line in the sand. "Taliban" he said again for two more stones, before placing them too on his battlefield. It looked like the enemy stones had all the advantage over the ANA stones who taking fire on three sides. Then the ANA counterattacked and ploughed the Taliban through the dirt as they were finger-pushed off the map.

"No Taliban", said the Afghan soldier as he casually flung stones into the irrigation canal.

After that first day at the culvert, I began to get accustomed to gunfire and learnt to tell what was close, what was overhead, what was accurate, and what was just "spray and pray". Nadi-Ali seemed to be busy and each day was accompanied by shooting, although the infantry always did a good job of protecting us as we worked slowly searching the road. With each opening burst of gunfire, the four of us would drop to the ground and then run back bent doubled over to the safety of the protecting Mastiff. We never saw any Taliban, only heard them fighting with our infantry. In my memory, Nadi Ali is blur of hot sunshine and dust and shooting. Some grew complacent. I'd just ran back behind the Mastiff that was creeping slowly behind us after a burst of firing, when I heard Smudge getting hysterical with Tom.

"Tom! Those are real fucking bullets you know! Get fucking doubling!" He was walking back with his Vallon over his shoulder and smoking a cigarette. Even now, I don't know what he was thinking.

The search that particular day had been to clear a road that a local tip off had indicated had an IED buried somewhere on it. We'd left the Mastiffs earlier and had searched all the way up this road when the firing began. It wasn't at us, but everyone was jumpy. Each time there was a burst of firing overhead, I could see Gibbs and Little Steve flinch into a half crouch before carrying on. It was in a residential area, so there were compounds on either side of the road, with alleyways running off each side every now and again. When you search, you are forced to walk slowly, while paying most of your attention to the ground you're about to walk on. It makes such a sitting duck. We have infantry a couple hundred metres off to our flanks on each side, but there was always the risk of Taliban being within the cordon, like what later happened on another search. Each alleyway you pass, you first stop and take a peek down it as you get in line, and keep your weapon pointing down it as you pass by. Just a group of kids standing there on the other end watching you. One of them waves before an old woman scolds them and they go running off. More firing to the left.

Eventually we got to the area where this IED was supposed to have been buried when we're told by our tangeeman the latest information from our tip-off. The Taliban had dug up the device, realising they'd been compromised and re-buried it somewhere else. That explained the hole we found later. It lay right at the bottom of an old IED crater. They'd actually buried another device in the crater of an old one. For a minute it looked like we'd be chasing this damn IED all around the green zone, but at that moment we realised we had stopped right outside a small shop. The shop owner sat outside against the wall with his legs drawn up in the customary way. There

was no emotion on his bearded face as he watched us and listened to the explosions in the distance. The day had been hot, dusty, full of flies, and there was still a lot of shooting up the road. Someone produced a wallet with US dollars and bought a few Cokes which were quickly passed around. No one is talking, everyone is sweating and guzzling and listening to the firing, while the local shop keeper goes back to his former squatting position.
There's been an Apache in the sky for a while now flying in slow, lazy orbits. The pilot was obviously trying to make head and tail of who was who in the contact below him, and he must have finally confirmed his targets because at that moment he fired a Hellfire missile. The massive bang gave everyone a chance to catch our breath as we finally stopped gulping, and ran outside to see what the hell that was. A black cloud of smoke was slowly creeping into the sky, and the shooting had abruptly stopped.
"I guess that's the end of them" someone said.
"That's come from the Apache. Hellfire" another guy replied, motioning to the chopper. "See, there's another one", and suddenly the air reverberates with another massive bang.
The Apache had arrived on the scene and at first had to work out where our soldiers were, where the locals were hiding and where the Taliban gun positions were. Once the pilot had worked all this out, the Taliban on the ground had seconds to live. Their only chance is to stay "air aware", hide and wait for the Apache to fly past before continuing the fight. In this case, they got caught red handed and like my friend had observed, that was the end of them. Well, a few of them at least. The survivors from the first explosion had been observed trying to carry some of their wounded to a vehicle that came to pick them up, only to all disappear in the second explosion.

I still remained scared whenever we went out on the ground, but after those first few searches I learnt to control the fear that can paralyse you. We were not out on the ground every day. Some days we got a lie in, not out of bed at four in the morning to be ready to go by five to be at a task by six. Instead, the Team would be on QRF. As a *Quick Reaction Force* day, also referred to as Admin Day, everyone gets some time to relax and catch up on the bare essentials, like slowly working our way through Season One of Gav and Stacey. As long as the team's kit is all squared away and ready to

go at short notice, we had the day to ourselves, provided nothing happened where troops beyond the walls need a Search Team.
Most times we got to catch up on sleep, before the daily supply helicopter arrived. It would come around eight o'clock every day, and would usually signal for people to get out of bed. Being my first tour, toilets were a bit of a shock to me. There was a cordoned off area with hollow boxes of wood and toilet seats fastened over holes in the centre of each one. You grab a wag-bag, always remembering to take some extra tissue paper from the ration boxes, open it up and hang it inside the hole, putting the toilet seat down over it.
Wag-bags are disposable, re-sealable plastic bags that have some sort of absorption crystals at the bottom, a bit like kitty litter. After you're done, you tuck it all in, seal it back up and throw it onto the burns pit on your way back. There was always alcohol gel on a table nearby. It was amazing how quickly this becomes normal.
If you want to urinate, that was far simpler. You just walk over to the row of plastic pipes- "desert roses" that are sticking out of the ground at an angle and pee into those.
The problem with relying on wag-bags each time you go to the toilet was that at that time there was a shortage for some reason. Each man was issued five bags a week, which meant that for two days a week we had to either hold in all bowel movements, or find another plastic bag like a black bin liner.
The bottled water was also rationed per man per week. Once you had finished your water, there was always the treated water to refill that two soldiers from the Royal Logistics Corps had set up. It tasted like chlorine, and that was why ration boxes came with powdered-juice.
I found that I knew one of those RLC guys. He was a black guy from South Africa, and we had been in basic training together. Somehow, he had ended up in the RLC and not the Engineers.
He had been sent to Shawquat to replace the last guy, who had been hit in the arm by the burns pit that you throw your carefully sealed, disgusting wag-bag. That bit of information suddenly gave me a dreadful thought, as I looked down at the piles of burst wag-bags spewing their half-burnt contents. I suddenly had the unsettling thought and asked, “did he fall *in* the burns pit when he was hit?" I think that would have been more traumatic than the actual gunshot. He gave a nervous laugh, then an awkward silence as we both simultaneously realised where we were standing.

I always made sure I gave that pit a wide berth when I passed by. I didn't want to be the next unlucky soldier to catch a stray bullet and end up falling into everyone's shit.

Search in itself can be either highly nerve racking, or very boring. Search Teams are different to *Barma* Teams because they only deal with the high threat areas, where it was quite likely IEDs will be buried. It could be because of a tip-off, or the peculiar behaviour of locals when using a stretch of road. It could be a channeled area like a culvert or gate-way. It could be someone spotting a firing hole off to the side, or some innocent looking sign: a hidden warning to locals not to go there. The list is endless. Barma Teams were the soldiers picked out to clear a road ahead of a convoy or a patrol. The route would still need to be searched, but as long as it was unlikely that there would be any hidden bombs planted in the road, the job would go to them. But when it came to something more threatening, when for any reason the commanders suspected there actually were going to be IED's, they will use the Search Team from the Engineers. High Risk High Assurance Search. We worked much slower, a lot more thoroughly and gave more attention. If the commander wanted a particular compound or firing point searched, then searchers will be the ones who have to make sure there are no hidden IED's for the infantry when they occupy it, or the sappers who fortify it. If there was a choke point in the road, like a wadi crossing point, or a bridge, then the Search Team would get called forward. The unspoken rule was you have to step on the ground if you've cleared it. You can't sweep your Vallon over a bit of earth and decide to move on and then step over it. There are soldiers walking behind you. If you say it's clear, then it's clear. Whenever the search team reaches a point in the road where the search ends, each man walks back down the route he just cleared, and you should be able to walk back up normally, without any care of getting blown to bits.

Each team gets a *RESA,* Royal Engineers Search Advisor, assigned to them. It would usually be an officer or senior NCO, and he's the man responsible for liaising with the commander the team is working with and advising them about how to go about things to eliminate IED threats, and how best to deploy the team.

A lot of the times, infantry commanders would try to offload tasks onto us in order to spare their own Barma Teams the risk of searching, and that's where our RESA would have to dig his heels in. High Risk Teams are for High Risk Areas. It was no good in over-working the searchers because they eventually start losing concentration in what they're doing, and that's when it got dangerous.

Our RESA, Troopie, reminded me of Lieutenant George in Black Adder Goes Forth. He was a lanky Irishman who initially came out with some fairly hair-brained ideas, but he genuinely cared about us. Often, he'd refuse to sleep in separate tents for the officers, and instead doss down with us. He would also never condescend to us. Even though we all knew we'd have to do what he said anyway, he had this habit of trying to explain things and convince us. In the Army, you get told what to do all the time, whether you like it or not, whether you understand it or not.

After the nightly O Group, after Troopie would stride in with his aerial photo and announced to his team what we would be doing the next day, after the knots in my stomach would begin,

I'd listen to the others discussing the next day's task from inside my doss bag, meanwhile going over the map details again in my head. The more I got used to picturing aerial photos, the easier it became to imagine it all. As I lie there, I can see the map features gradually transform from shiny plastic to real life, and begin to wonder what would be the best way to successfully kill someone with a home-made bomb. I'd use deception. I'd keep them guessing, keep them scared. I'd imagine the panic they must feel when trying to get a wounded comrade out, most likely making a bee line to safety without thinking of the consequences of not thinking. And I'd place another bomb in that place too.

In the night, another distant, dull boom goes unnoticed.

It can take hours, even days to clear roads, and after that it has to be watched continuously. If even for five minutes there has been no one guarding it, then it's too risky. The Taliban are very good at laying IEDs quickly. It has to be searched again, just as thoroughly the second time. No one can set foot anywhere without searching it. Soldiers from earlier tours where IEDs were much less of a threat had come back with exciting stories of pitched battles with the Taliban, making others who had not yet been deployed quietly jealous and impatient.

My deployment came conveniently at a time when Taliban usage of IED's had gone up 600%. What that meant for the soldiers fighting on the ground was that no longer can commanders send their men bounding across open ground as if they're on Salisbury Plain or dominating the high ground. It had to be searched. Everywhere had to be searched. When they get ambushed, they take a massive risk when they dive into the nearest ditch for cover, because that's where the Taliban had pre-buried their booby-traps. I knew of some soldiers who preferred staying on the road and risk getting hit than crawling into dead ground because as frightening as gunfire is, it's nothing compared with an explosion.

You lie there awake at night, thinking of ways you could die out here. You can drown trapped in a Mastiff at the bottom of an irrigation canal. You can get shot in an ambush, as you walk slowly along. You can get gunned down while you sleep by the ANA or ANP who didn't care about defecting to the Taliban, but were instead harboring a grudge against you. Your helicopter can be shot down as it flies you to your latest destination. But by far the worst, and most common method of death and injury is to get blown up from below. You wear body armor and a helmet to protect you from incoming rounds, and a lot of soldier's have been saved by them. But there's nothing to protect you from the violence erupting upwards from between your legs. Most of my war-experience was spent being wary of walking anywhere.

"Where did you get the knife from?" one of us asked.

"I killed a Taliban and took it off him" said our tangeeman.

That unexpected bit of information grabbed everyone's attention. Our interpreter that day spoke very good English with a slight American accent, and said he once worked for the U.N. until he punched another man in the mouth for being an Uzbek. It lost him his job.

"A lot of the interpreters are not allowed to carry weapons, but this commander gave me one," he explained. "We were on patrol a few days ago and passed a Taliban, but they did not know. But I saw him

and when he saw me looking at him, he started running away. So I shot him three times and later took this knife off his body".
He seemed a pretty normal man to me, sitting there playing with a kitten that had wandered over to our group. He had a slight build and was softly spoken, like a university type. Not at all someone who I'd expect to go blurting out how he had just brassed-up some Chohgee on a gut feeling.
There were fourteen of us lounging around in the sun inside the walled compound of whoever's home it had once been. We'd crashed at the nearest check point and helped the infantry with stag that night because armoured transport had been unable to get us back to the FOB the previous day. I'd been drinking too much water the day before and was now having to go easy on what I had left.
Our tangeeman was an educated man, who seemed to have his own opinion about the war. As we sat there with him, the conversation turned a bit deeper.
"So…why is Afghanistan like this?" someone eventually asked.
We'd all wondered this as soon as we landed in the country – coming from a world of Jedward, Skype and Youtube, to…this. Stinking irrigation ditches. Mud compounds, donkey-drawn wagons, and people basically living like they had been living a thousand years ago with absolutely no idea what they were missing out on.
"Afghanistan is not all like this," he explained. "If you go to Kabul, you will find shopping malls, even escalators."
After a few weeks of wading chest high in smelly irrigation water and sleeping on the ground with chickens darting all over the place, this revelation came as a surprise.
"It's just Helmand" he said. "Well, maybe a few other parts too."
"Okay, so why is Helmand like this?" asked Little Steve.
"Cos they're idiots" he said, stroking the kitten behind the ears. It had a mouse in its jaws, still alive.
"They don't get any education here, so they actually believe what the Taliban say,"
"Maybe if we gave them all TVs, they'd just stay in and binge watch Game of Thrones," I suggested.
I'd seen my first real live IED the previous day. It had been discovered by the ANA, in a residential area. It was right in the middle of the road, placed to tear through the centre of a vehicle. The ANA had noticed a wire running off the side of the road, into

the bushes along the wall of a compound. Someone had been crouching around the corner of the wall, waiting for a vehicle to come by before he was spotted and ran away. The soldiers then performed a bit of EOD of their own – they cut the wire so no one could send any electricity to the explosives, which was a very brave thing to do because if it was another type of device, that would have been the last thing they did.

Just to make double sure there was not another wire leading to it, we decided to check around it anyway before Jim could deal with the thing. As we walk, we made sure that no command wires were buried leading into the area from off to one side, because that would mean someone was sitting on the other end of the wire, waiting to kill Jim.

In this case, we had deep irrigation ditches on each side of the road, followed immediately by a high mud wall which did not let us give it a wide berth if it did explode. In the end we decided to simply walk around the device, really quickly.

The main charge was in a yellow oil drum sitting snug in a neat hole, and the top had been uncovered for us to each get a look at it as we walked around. I couldn't believe I was seeing a real IED. A real bomb, that makes real explosions. It was like looking down from a boat and seeing dorsal fin in the ocean below you. Always signs of Taliban, but never Taliban.

"The problem with the war here," the tangeeman continued, "is if you kill one of the Taliban, the mother will tell the children that ISAF killed their father. Then they will grow up knowing only that ISAF killed my father. It doesn't matter what ISAF has done for their country. They will fight you too."

Then Troopie asked a question. "But what about all the money and aid we have been giving to Afghanistan? What about the schools and clinics?"

"That doesn't matter to them," he explained. Then he said something I'll always remember. "You can give someone $100,000, and he will take your money, buy a home, start a business, and have a family. Then, after he has done all that, he will still come back and fight you."

The massacre that made headlines on SKY and BBC news happened that day just down the road from we were guarding a road. The main

effort had been to meet up with some local leaders for a *Shura*, a meeting. It had taken all morning to get to the location. Like anywhere in Helmand, the road had to be searched first and then piqueted by Mastiffs dropping off the tail of the convoy every five hundred metres, pulling over to the side of the road into a searched lay-by, switch off the engines and watch the road. For the Search Team somehow crammed into two of those Mastiffs, it was going to be a long day. My initial fear of getting blown into the adjacent canal and drowning inside the Mastiff were relieved when it was our turn to drop off and guard the road. I had mixed feelings about travelling in Mastiffs. There were only two ways out – the gun turret, and the back exit. Everyone has to clamber through the length of the vehicle from the rear, encumbered by their body armour getting caught by bits of kit stored in every nook and cranny. Ammo tins for the .50 calibre machine gun in the gun turret, ECM, radios. All the search team's kit, rifles. It's like being in a little submarine. About ten soldiers had crawled in, somehow managing to find storage places for the paraphernalia that accompanies every man and then somehow managing to configure the spaghetti knot of limbs into some kind of comfy arrangement. And there you sit, strapped into the seat. You can turn your head, and move your arms, but the rest of your body is strapped in tightly to prevent you from smashing your head into the ceiling if the vehicle should blow up. Although plenty of Mastiffs had been blown up by IED's, none had actually been able to penetrate the armour.
One of the two main dangers of travelling by Mastiff was getting violently thrown around inside, or getting hit by a bit of kit not secured properly. Before soldiers are deployed out on the ground, they undergo a series of last-minute induction lectures like tourniquet applying, getting on and off helicopters without getting chopped in half by the rotors or shot by their flares. One of the stands was the Mastiff Stand. We gathered around a vehicle that had been involved in a contact IED. The explosion must have been enormous. Both of the front wheels and axle had been torn off, and it was sitting on the ground at an angle. The NCO who took that quick induction lesson went through all the basic facts about a Mastiff, pointing out how the IED had not penetrated the armour.
"One thing you must remember," he told our small group. "Always make sure you use these seat belts. I've just finished cleaning all the

blood and bits of hair out of this Mastiff because someone sitting in it wasn't strapped in."
It was a sobering comment.

The other threat was from the canals. A dominant feature of Nad-i-Ali was the network of irrigation ditches that criss-crossed the region. They ranged from thigh deep channels that we were forever wading through when searching for command wires, to enormous rivers that could easily swallow up a vehicle as large as a Mastiff. The Taliban must have grown tired of scoring direct hits on Mastiffs, only to watch dazed survivors staggering out of the smoke. They came up with the ingenious idea of blowing the vehicle from the side, into the water. It had been attempted before, and after the scene of the explosion had been investigated after the incident, it was pretty clear what their plan had been. Several Mastiffs have rolled on their own accord, when the driver had gone too near the edge, or when the road had collapsed under the weight. I know of one soldier who was decorated for dragging drowned passengers out from the underwater wreck and reviving them with CPR. Very, very brave man.
I wasn't brave. Riding slowly along the road, trying not to think about explosions, or tangled seatbelts that won't undo, or rolling, or drowning in panicky black darkness, ears ringing, head smashed against ceilings, upside down, filling up with water. I was sitting in the front seat, next to the driver. We'd both have the furthest to crawl. Once again, I was trying not to think about any of this for two kilometres until suddenly our vehicle edged over to the side into a searched box. The relief.
That day was quiet and peaceful. No shooting. No explosions. Around us were green fields with wind carving waves in the long grass. Chohgees were dotted here and there carrying on with their business. Five hundred metres up the road was another Mastiff, like a pillbox in a sea of green. The gunner would be sitting behind his HMG[5] getting bored of watching out for anyone digging holes in the road.
Inside these vehicles, people were sweating. Crosswords were being shared around in the back, and iPod batteries were slowly getting

[5] Heavy machine gun

drained. The sweat starts under your helmet where your soaked hair cannot hold any more liquid. It forms beads below your saturated sweat band and suddenly streams down your temples and neck, under your Osprey[6], where it joins the sweat that your shoulders and back created, then seeps down to collect at your belt. You squirm in your seat, and like a long aeroplane trip, suddenly no position is comfortable anymore. Behind me is the gunner, though all you can see of him are his legs as he stands on his gun platform.
Occasionally wafts of fresh air would blow into the vehicle, and you can feel it on your skin for a split second.
After three hours of guarding the road, my iPod battery had at last ran out so there was to be no more Jimi Hendrix that day. I put on the headset of the radio and had a listen to the net. The driver and gunner both had a radio fixed to their heads with a mouth piece. It's called a PRR – Personal Role Radio – and it's an easy way to communicate with each other. But there's always another ear-piece which resembles a telephone, and that's what I was holding to my ear, leaning against the side like someone back in the UK on his mobile while driving. Sometimes you'd hear other call-signs in the area talking to each other, but that also gets boring. Still, it was better than listening to all the snoring and smelling the farts and body odour that was coming from the back.
I don't remember what exactly was said that caught our attention, but I do remember the driver and I both looking at each other in alarm.
"Times three ISAF KIA, times three Cat-A." A Category A injury is very serious. "Blue 2-5…."
"Blue 2-5 under contact"
The driver took his glasses off and swore. "What is going on over there?"
"Where is Blue 2-5?" I asked.
"Just down the road, back the way we came" he said, looking out the bullet proof window. "That way."
"Blue 2-5 under contact from within" the net was saying.
"You're kidding me?" I said, genuinely startled. "They're getting over-run?!"
The voices over the net were charged with emotion. Several people

[6] Body armour

were communicating, and the casualty figures had gone up. "Times four KIA." Someone was saying to calm down and please repeat, over.
"Everyone is flapping." said the driver. We sat there in silence, listening to the unfolding drama. By now, people in the back had been told what was happening just down the road. Gibbs was the next man sitting behind me, and I would repeat any major developments onto him.
The casualties had gone up. Five killed. More had been wounded, including one ANP who I remember being mentioned as "shot in the leg". No one could hear gunfire, it was still a sunny, peaceful day. Only it was not really peaceful. In a compound not far away, men were dying. Others were trying their best to remember their training and keep the wounded alive until help arrived. No doubt everyone sitting in their Mastiffs along the road that day were listening quietly to the net, wondering what had gone wrong. Had the Taliban really over-run a checkpoint? Those nights, sleeping under the stars in compounds, taking your turn at stag, crouched behind a machine gun at two in the morning wondering if that shadow really is moving. Never seeing anyone.

We later got the whole story that evening when we finally got back to the FOB. Five men had been killed. Others were wounded, including some ANP. It had been one of their own. One of the ANP, who I heard had recently been sacked for being unreliable and generally dodgy had proceeded to prove how unreliable and dodgy he was by simply letting himself into his old check-point and begin shooting. The soldiers at that moment had had all their body armour off and were caught completely off guard. One of the men had seen what was about to happen and went straight for the former policeman, trying to punch him before a burst of gunfire killed him. The ANP man then went on a rampage, shooting British soldiers and his former ANP colleagues before getting away.
We listened to all these details that evening back at the FOB. We were sitting in the tent, having just strode in from the Mastiff park and dumped all our kit and took off our Osprey. It wasn't too long before the tannoy system interrupted the conversation. Tannoy systems were always difficult to make out because of the echo. "Stand by for broadcast-cast-cast-ast…all team medics-medics-

edics-dics….report to the Med Centre-centre-entre-tre…all team medics-medics-edics-dics….report to the Med Centre-centre-entre-tre…end of broadcast-cast-cast-ast."

At the Med centre, a crowd of soldiers had already gathered. Latex gloves were being passed out and groups of friends were clumped here and there all talking in subdued voices about what had happened, and who had been killed. I listened, trying to put names to faces. It turned out that a few of the dead had been the same guys who had been part of our cordon the previous day when we had dealt with the IED in the road. The one where the ANA had cut the command wire themselves. The Regimental Sergeant Major, the big guy I had passed on my first day out on the ground, he was dead too. I had later heard that he personally guarded that IED overnight, making sure no one came to retrieve it before we detonated it safely in the middle of a field.

Just outside the entrance to the med centre was a stretcher elevated off the ground, and on it was a figure lying very, very still. The skin was all drained and looked whiter than normal in the half-light, and in disbelief I came out with a pretty stupid comment.

"Is that…a…*mannequin*?" I asked out loud before I could stop myself, straining my eyes to get a better look. It was just lying there, so still on the stretcher. For a moment, I had no idea what I was saying, or what a mannequin would be doing on a Forward Operating Base in Helmand. Maybe it was one of those dummies that the med centre might keep to train soldiers how to give CPR and other first aid drills.

Smudge looked at me, shaking his head slowly in frustration. It looked like he was going to say something, but instead decided to just leave it. The mannequin on the stretcher moved slightly as the pretty doctor came out with her sleeves rolled up and latex gloves on. American medics helped her as she examined a swab of bandages wrapped around the patient's stomach. He was an Afghan who had also been shot in the compound that day, but it didn't seem like he was aware of much as he lay there under the stars, waiting for the chopper to take him back to the surgeons at Bastion.

Off to the other side of the Med centre, in the shadows, were the body bags. Everyone was trying not to talk about them though they were subtly pointed out. One of the senior NCO's spoke up, instructing us to organise ourselves into stretcher parties and carry

the body bags over to the HLS[7]. Each group carried their load with delicate care, determined to protect them from any type of bump or knock. We waited there for the approaching Chinook, hearing the distant *thwump thwump thwump* of the massive rotors get louder.
I'm standing with the others, helmet on, eye goggles obscuring my vision and trying to ignore the solid feeling against my leg. Thinking about the last time I saw them alive. Here comes the Chinook, landing. A blast of wind and stones. We're shuffling along now, waiting our turn to move forward. The loadmaster motions us onto the ramp, gently does it. Lower him carefully alongside the others.
Later that night, everyone is to parade by the ops room. There we were told by the CO what had happened, though by now everyone knows. He told us the names of who had been killed, and when he got to the RSM, he stopped and seemed to choke up. They had been old friends. He went on to say that a massive man-hunt was in place to track down the former ANP man who did it. He mentioned that the Taliban would also be trying to find him before we do, that it was their hope that this kind of incident would serve to drive a wedge between us and our Afghan allies.
"You're all highly trained soldiers" he said. "We can't afford for you to lose focus, so keep an eye on each other for behaviour changes. If you notice your oppo isn't going to the gym anymore or isn't eating, let your section commanders know."
Naturally, the Taliban later claimed that the entire incident had been their plan all along, but no one really cared what they claimed.
That day was a rude awakening. Death is real, and it can come from any angle when you least expect it. The fact that I had seen those men just a few days previously made the whole incident seem a lot closer. For the rest of the tour, I was always weary of the Afghan soldiers and policemen, which may seem unfair on them because most of them had joined the army because the Taliban had killed their relatives and they hated them with a passion.
I later signed out a pistol the next time we were at the armoury at Bastion and reconfigured the pouches attached to my body armour to keep it, along with all the kit Searchers have to carry. Those poor guys in their body bags must have felt safe when they finally

---

[7] Helicopter landing site

returned from their foot patrol and took off their body armour.

We're searching another compound. It's been quiet today, with very little shooting every now and again. We been walking around the walls to make sure no command wire ran into it to blow us up, and finally we began searching the compound itself. It's going to take all day. Gibbs and I are working on one wall, sweeping our Vallons up and down in large swathes to detect any potential IED buried within it. It's slow progress, and burns your arms after a while, but this is one of those things that had to be done thoroughly. Gibbs is further on up the wall, working his way from that corner to the middle, and I'm working my way from my corner to meet him. I had bent over to carefully remove a rock, and sweat drips rapidly from my eyebrows onto the inside of my ballistic glasses. My world is momentarily blurred, eyes stinging. There's little wind, and loads of flies. I'd just yelled at Gibbs not to go wondering off too far down when a sudden single burst of gunfire sends me flat on the ground. Its very loud.
I look up. Gibbs is sprinting towards me, flat out. Without even realising it, I'm back on my feet and sprinting too. There's a funny EOD joke I had seen on the back of tour t-shirts. 'EOD: If You See Me Running, Try To Catch Up!' I don't know why, but this was what was flashing through my mind as I'm sprinting along the wall. Not 'I'm going to die', or 'please God let me live.' Instead, it's that stupid T-shit with the joke written on the back. I didn't even know where I was running to, or why. All I had heard was loud cracks, and seen Gibbs legging it, so I did the same
Big Steve was on the road by the Mastiff. He didn't know why we were running either. "What's up with you two?" he asked. This was now the second time this sort of thing has happened to me.
"I ran cos he ran" I said, breathless. "You didn't hear that?"
"What's up, Gibbs?" he said as Gibbs came trotting in, looking behind him. It was back to being all quiet again.
"You didn't see that?! I nearly got shot!" he said, catching his breath. He was grinning, a mixture between genuinely shocked and ecstatic. "There were rounds landing all around me!"
"I didn't see anything", said Big Steve. "Did you?"
"No, I didn't see anything" I said "but dived from that last bit of shooting, then look up and see Gibbs sprinting towards me. So, I ran

too."
I could understand the hint of excitement, even joy at having been shot at. Every soldier trains for combat. Training and training and training to react professionally under fire, only to never actually get shot at is like those poor Cold War era government agents who knew the launch codes and trained and trained and trained to do something that in the end never happened.
Later on, we found out who had pulled the trigger. It was from further up the road. Some ANA checkpoint had opened up on a Chohgee on a motorbike who had failed to stop. Some of the rounds they fired at him had gone whizzing past, to land at the feet of a soldier who was at that moment giving a three-metre high wall his undivided attention.

The compound we had been busy searching was owned by an Afghan family. They didn't know it at the time, but they were about to lose their home. Earlier that day, they had shown us typical hospitality when their fifteen-year-old son had emerged from the house with some freshly baked bread and placed it in the middle of the yard, motioning us to help ourselves.
Chohgee bread is delicious, especially when it just came out the oven and still hot. The Search Team had just finished clearing the entire compound, and we were at last relaxing in the adjacent courtyard. Everyone's body armour has been taken off, spread out on the ground and used as an improvised mattress. Gibbs and Little Steve were asleep in the shade of a wall. A lot of us were. I was looking up at the sky, wondering what was going to happen. Just before we had finished the compound search, locals sitting on a tractor had chugged by, pulling imaginary triggers and pointing up the road. Other people who had travelled up that way were now all coming back and told our tangeeman what we had already figured out from the trigger-finger symbols. There was an ambush up ahead. It was just as well we weren't going that way anyway. Our job had been to make sure there were no devices in the compound before the sappers showed up to transform the place into a fortified military checkpoint.
The tangeeman came through the small gap in the wall, looking all excited.
"In maybe five minutes, there will be much shooting. Taliban over

there," he says, waving over the wall. As soon as he said that, there's this sudden burst of gunfire, followed immediately by a single, solid detonation. You can feel the air move slightly. Then silence. Those who were asleep are awake, still lying on their backs in the sun, dozily asking what that was all about.
"Taliban ambush up the road."
There was another loud explosion.
"Those might have been own goals" someone reckoned. We had no call-signs up there. There were no Apaches in the area.
We later found out what had happened. The ambushers had laid IEDs in the road before taking up position and lying in wait, only someone must have forgotten where not to step, and scored an "own goal". The second explosion had been their casevac[8] getting blown to pieces.
I went back to sleep.

Later that day, the combat engineers started to arrive, with a medium wheelie and all the building materials they would need for their work that night. The family whose home this was grew quieter and quieter while they looked on at this latest development. I think they had already guessed what going to happen even before an officer went over to their group with an interpreter. They spoke for a long time, all sitting cross legged on the ground in a circle. Around us, the noise of a construction site invaded the quiet rural day. Heavy duty machinery was manoeuvring into place and *Beep! Beep! Beep!* reversing noises were interrupting the little *shura* that was taking place with the family. They watched as a section of wall came toppling down to make the front gate.
None of us liked what was happening. We felt sheepish, like we had deceived these people. That they had baked bread for us made it all the worse. We had no way of telling them in advance what was going to happen, because the Taliban would have found out and then there *would* have been IEDs everywhere. On the other hand, it had been decided that to make this a safer area, some sort of military presence needed to be established to make sure no one dug anything into the roads at night. That meant a check point.

[8] Casualty evacuation

A little later the shura ended. A deal must have been struck, which usually involved a chit with which the family could hand in to ISAF authorities in exchange for a sum of money. In our opinion, it came nowhere near to a home. We helped them move their enormous mound of harvested corn away from the construction site that the corner of their home had turned into.

The Afghans have a clever way of carrying large amounts of crops. They undo a length of cloth which is usually wrapped around their heads, and let it trail down their backs, like a long ponytail. Then they gather a big bundle of corn stalks, pass the strip of cloth underneath the bundle, pulling it up on the other side towards them. This lifts up the load onto their backs, and off they go with their cargo, bent forward slightly, one hand out for balance and the other hand grasping the cord.

All the men in the family went to work efficiently in this manner, making quick work of their summer harvest. An old man who must have been over seventy and carrying a load his size walked briskly past one of our soldiers, who had his arms full of a pathetic looking collection of corn, half of which was escaping between his legs and trailing behind him.

"ISAF – we're here to help!" joked Big Steve. It had become a common joke to quote the official ISAF slogan each time the military screwed up something for a neighbourhood.

By now, the first wall of hesco had been established, and was being worked on by two muscled Fijians, stripped to the waist, and levelling out the sand with shovels. Around the corner, keeping watch was another one of the combat engineers behind a minimi[9]

Our group stayed out of the way, our job of checking the area for booby traps done. We were all strung out along a wall, eating our rations for dinner, and waiting to be told what was going to happen with us. I didn't want to stay there anymore.

Eventually we were told we'd be spending the night in another compound down the road. As we left in single file, I remember the look of the fifteen-year-old as I walked by him, the same boy who had offered us bread earlier that day. He stared at me as I walked past him. Such scorn. I'll never forget it.

I remembered a quote from the Vietnam War, how one American

---

[9] Light machinegun

soldier described how they liberated a hamlet from the communists. "We had to destroy the village in order to save it."
That was a bit like what was happening here, I thought. To make their home safer, we're taking it from them.
But I didn't say anything.

We lay in our doss bags that night, looking up at the stars. They were incredible. The night sky was pitch black, without any city lights in the distance. It wasn't cold yet, and the evenings were still warm enough to sprawl out with your head rested on outstretched hands and listen to the sounds of the surrounding local neighbourhood. Dogs were barking, women were shouting for their children. People actually lived here, I thought.
Before I knew it, I was being woken up for my turn at stag up on the flat roof of one of the mud huts. The only other person awake was someone sitting by the radio listening to the net, and he had the stag list, with where each man was sleeping. For two hours on the roof, I crouch behind the machine gun with my own rifle beside me and scanning the ground every so often through the night vision. A peaceful, starry night.

First the breaking of dawn over the horizon, sunrays streaming across the pink and orange sky. Then the explosion.
The sudden, solid boom rocked the morning air. Everyone stops eating breakfast. It came from the compound we had cleared the day before. I was sitting next to Gibbs.
"Oh fuck..."
"IED?" It's what everyone is thinking.
"We missed something?" I felt sick. Oh God. Oh God oh God oh God oh God. Whose area was it in? Was it me? Did I miss it?
A few of the infantry had gotten to their feet, and the man on the roof on stag was looking at the compound through the scope of his rifle.
"It's alright lads," announced the radio operator. "RPG. Airburst."
It seemed that the Taliban down the road were still there. They'd fired an RPG over the compound the sappers had spent all night and all morning working on. It exploded in the air above them. There were no casualties.

We're on another QRF day, though there's not going to be any admin because we have to accompany another convoy to some patrol base a few kilometers away. A Forward Operating Base, or FOB, would usually be at the heart of a network of smaller outposts, known as PB's. Patrol Bases. Outposts get smaller and more spartan with Check-points - CP's. Most FOBs by the time I entered the war had a decent standard of living. Soldiers live in ten-man tents, with electricity for lap-top based movies, camp-cots, and a cookhouse usually providing fresh hot evening meals. Shawquat's shower system was still reliant on solar bags that you need to heat up all day to get any warm water, but at least every man could have one shower every second day. That was quite good. There was always a couple of dusty, beaten-up laptops available for half-hour internet slots, with soldiers patiently waiting their turn. Some of the keys would be missing, leading to some interesting misunderstandings in emails over the months.
Patrol Bases and Check Points are a lot more basic. They're basically compounds taken over for the use of their thick high wall which already gives decent cover. If there's a building, you're in luck because otherwise your bed space will be anywhere that's out of the way. Unless some engineers are in the area, you probably won't have any shower areas and you have to improvise with wet wipes to wipe the sweat off your back to prevent prickly heat. Some Patrol Bases are more developed and resemble FOBs. Actually, I never was sure if there was any defining feature that makes a FOB a FOB, and a PB a PB. All that mattered to me when harbored up somewhere over night was the water-situation, the stag-list, and what time reveille was in the morning.

The Patrol Base we had spent a few hours slowly driving to was under attack. The driver and gunner could hear it on the net and spread the word to the rest of us. The gunners in the Mastiffs up ahead began opening up when they got some sort of target indication over the radios, while their drivers maneuvered into position, careful to keep within the searched area and not to stray off onto any IEDs. The HMG above us exploded into life briefly, then fell silent. The gunner was adjusting his sights. Then he began pouring it on. One of the IEDD lads was sitting uncomfortably underneath him, getting hot brass falling on him as the spent cartridges were ejected from the machine gun and glittering down into the vehicle. He would jerk with an "*aaargh!*" every now and then.

For the rest of us inside those Mastiffs, it was another case of sit tight and let the heavy weaponry take care of things. Each man is armed with a rifle, but they're really just pea-shooters. I could just about see out of the thick front windows, and also the driver's digital camera screen. Mastiffs are so large and difficult to drive that they have cameras covering different sides of the vehicle. The images are fed back to a big TV screen that the driver can pull down in front of him and watch each camera's images so he knows his position, or what's behind him.

Between the windows and the cameras, I could build up an image of what outside looked like. To the right was an irrigation canal. The patrol base lay about fifty meters away, just over a culvert. A couple of Mastiffs were up ahead, shooting into thick tall grass, higher than a man. The patrol base itself consisted of a mud wall, with bits of corrugated iron roofing emerging here and there. There was a solitary tower with a sanger at the top, draped with camouflage netting flapping lazily in the wind. A single step ladder led up to the top. From what our Troopie was telling us, the fire coming from the Taliban was pretty accurate, and there were a couple of lads trapped up in the sanger and were getting ammunition tossed up to them from other soldiers in the courtyard to keep the machine gun shooting.

This was all interesting information, but secretly I was just glad I didn't have to go out there. It sounded like there was a *lot* of shooting going on the other side of the thick armored door. The machine gun above us was firing in bursts. *DUFF-DUFF-DUFF.... DUFF-DUFF-DUFF-DUFF!* Hot brass cartridges were tingling down, scorching people below who were patiently crossing their legs and holding it in.

Someone grinned and asked "Does anyone else need to piss?"

A few of us looked up from the communal crossword-puzzle book and nodded our agreement, clearly not impressed with not being able to go outside because of the contact. I was getting a bit bored. Like every other time spent sitting in a Mastiff the entire day, I was sitting in my own sweat, hot and dusty, constantly needing to pick my dusty nose, and beginning to fantasize about unbuckling my seatbelt,

swinging open those heavy doors, ripping my body armor off and diving into the cool irrigation channel. I didn't care how muddy it was.
DUFF DUFF DUFF DUFF DUFF DUFF DUFF!
It was then that it became apparent that something needed to happen. Well, at least for the man sitting opposite me. He was in the Royal Artillery, and apart from resupplying the PB, he was another reason why we had come. Some system to do with coordinating artillery support had broken down, and he was the guy sent to have a look at it and see if he could get it working again. The problem, at least for him, was the distance to cover into the PB. It was open ground, over the culvert, and into the open back gates. Him and I were both sitting at the back seats, right by the entrance.
"Open up the door just a bit," Troopie was telling me, then turned to the Repair Guy "make sure you wait for the gunner to pop some smoke first."
I looked over at Repair Guy. He was very, very quiet. Chewing some gum. I was feeling sorry for him, but also still relieved it wasn't me who was having to run out into all that. I pulled up the handle, and pushed the heavy door open slightly, letting in some cool fresh air. The noise level increased instantly. Lots of crackling and snapping.
DUF-DUF-DUF-DUF-DUF.
"You okay mate?" I asked him. He carried on chewing his gum, didn't say anything. Just carried on staring at the PB gates.
The gunner had thrown a smoke grenade, it goes sailing over and lands fairly central in the ground that Repair Guy has to cover. Orange smoke starts streaming out, and Repair Guy makes a movement.
"Woah, wait for it to build up," I say, blocking the entrance with my arm. The smoke gets a down draft, getting slowly blown into the ground. The two Mastiffs disappear and immediately Repair Guy is gone, like a race horse. I see him sprinting through the smoke and at the same time lean out to heave the armored door shut.
It was then that the unthinkable happened. My Hoodlum fell out. A Hoodlum is a hand-held metal detector, not unlike the ones they sweep over your body at the airport. I always kept mine hanging off the front of my osprey in easy reach and as I leaned forward, my thigh must have pushed it up to unhook it. It fell, in slow motion. Onto my boot. Bounced. Onto the step, bounced again. Wafts of

orange smoke, giving that unique smoke grenade smell. Hit the ground, bounced. *DUF-DUF-DUF-DUF-DUF* (will it ever stop bouncing!?) and finally came to a halt.
I nervously turned to Troopie. I couldn't quite believe how quickly events had just changed. "Sir, my, er, Hoodlum fell out". At the time, it didn't seem like my mind was working. All I could think about was the noises coming from outside. I needed someone to tell me what to do. My stomach felt bottomless.
"Well, go out and get it," Troopie says, bemused.
Now I'm stuck. I got no choice.
Without thinking about it, I'm suddenly outside, heart in my mouth. The Hoodlum is in my hand, with dirt I had just clawed out of the ground, hear a crack, hear an embarrassing noise escape my lips, and now I'm flying through the air, front leg out stretched, grabbing onto the bar armor, why the hell are these doors so heavy? Bang my knee on the step. Grate my shin. Now I'm sitting back down where I had been three seconds ago. Big Steve is struggling to breathe, he's laughing so hard.
Troopie's grinning, slowly shaking his head. "I've never seen you move so fast! That was just incredible."
The firing stopped not too long afterwards. By that time, a lot of people in the Mastiffs must have been dying to relieve themselves, because slowly soldiers began emerging cautiously from the rear of their vehicles, grinning at each other and giving the 'rock on' sign with their free hand while urinating against a tire. Someone was emptying a plastic bottle of urine before it was mistaken for apple juice. Big Steve was the first one out of our vehicle. There were still a few parting shots in the distance, but it didn't stop him from sneaking over to the side of a building and doing his business. The memories of my last excursion out of the vehicle were still fresh in my mind, so I opted to sit it out just a little while longer, until I saw for myself that he was safely back in his seat. Only then was I convinced I could also go to the toilet without risking my life. I was half surprised I had not wet myself when I ran out to get my Hoodlum, I was that desperate. I had heard of plenty of other people wetting themselves in that sort of situation without even noticing until much later.

One day it stopped being hot. A steady wind was blowing, and it was overcast. The next day was the same, and from then on winter set in. Whenever we were spending the night at FOB Shawquat, we had to adhere to the strict rules in place there. You still had to shave every day, and keep side burns up. Shaving had become quite painful for me, because I was running out of razor blades. I had no electric razors, so was relying on using the cheap plastic razors that civilians had sent out to soldiers in care packages. They were very painful. The rule was that you were not allowed in the cook house to get a hot dinner if you had not shaved. As my last two blades began getting blunter, I came up with a solution to the hot water shortage. The water set aside for ablutions would never get a chance to get even luke-warm because of the number of soldiers using it, and replacing it with unheated water. Its agony shaving in cold water with blunt razors blades, but I eventually began stealing small Styrofoam cups of hot water from the coffee urn. From then on, every evening a plastic cup full of hot water would disappear from the cookhouse and end up in the ablutions area.

The showers were in the open air as well. When the Afghan winter began setting in, this also became a problem, especially when the solar bags which had been lying in the sun all day were not warm enough. Soldiers with towels around their waists would make their way to the showers, holding a solar bag half filled with warmish water, if they were lucky. You suspend it from an overhead beam, hang your towel up and loosen the nozzle. Sharp intake of breath as the icy water trickles down over you. The guy in the next shower is making similar noises. In about five minutes, as little time as possible, you have washed off the sweat and grime from the last two days and you're no longer smelling of body odor. Your hair isn’t hard and matted anymore. You go to sleep feeling really, really good.

All our laundry was done by hand. Beside the shower area, tables were set up and that was where we washed all our kit in two big basins - one for lathering, one for rinsing. Usually, we kept a set of kit clean by wearing it only after we had a chance to wash our bodies, and sleeping in it. All our other clothes were the ones we had to wash all the time, the ones we waded through muddy water in, or the ones we sweated in all day cooped inside a Mastiff. There would always be soldiers there during Admin Days doing their best at hand washing. No matter how much shampoo I swamped those clothes in, or how many times I rinsed, the water I poured away would always be black. No one ever really got rid of that smell.

Sometimes when we had been away from the main base for a few days, I would get so sweaty and dirty beneath my U-back, that prickly heat would begin to spread across my back, because of the clogged pores of skin. The slightest touch or scrape would set the skin on fire with a prickling, burning, itching sensation that made wearing the heavy body armor a small prison. Wherever we were, we made sure to keep wet wipes with us. Wet wipes became worth their weight in gold and were always used sparingly. One would be used for the face. Two were used for the shoulders and back, which was where prickly heat usually struck. One would be used for your groin, and one more for each armpit. Each paper tissue would come away creased with black dirt and sweat, and tossed onto a fire.

Smudge and I got prickly heat the worst and had to get some special cream from the med-center at the corner of the camp. We took turns rubbing it into each other's backs, joking about it as we did so.

"Just think of it as a bonding experience," said Smudge. He had his eyes closed and was enjoying the back rub I was giving him. Soon it was my turn for a back rub. After the cream was rubbed in, the itchiness soon began to disappear. Each time we had the cream on we tried going for as long as possible without our shirts, without lying down or leaning against anything which might rub it off. When it did come to finally putting on a top for dinner, we did so with the greatest care.

There was another problem with spending the coming winter in Shawquat. None of us had the right dress to queue up for the cookhouse in the evenings back at the FOB. The Grenadiers, being a Guards Regiment, were particularly fussy about appearances like being cleanly shaven, having short sideburns, and wearing the correct army jacket when lining up at the cookhouse. The only alternative allowed was wearing our U-backs, which were paper thin and not designed for insulation.

We discovered this during the first evening when it suddenly began to get cold. No one had brought the standard issued jackets that have to be worn in barracks across the UK. Instead, we queued up for our dinner wearing the special issued winter softies[10] that soldiers

receive for Afghanistan. At the front of the queue, one of the senior NCOs approached our group, gesturing at our incorrect dress.
"You're not allowed them in here, fellas," he said. A quiet growl of annoyance went through the team. Engineers hate being called 'fella,' though being in the Grenadiers, the NCO must not have realized.
"What?" asked Smudge in disbelief.
"Only smocks or shirts are allowed for dinner," he explained. It looked like he was aware of how ridiculous it was to be enforcing dinner dress codes on soldiers who might have nearly been killed that day, or might be killed the next. But he loyally stuck with it. The Grenadiers were in charge of Shawquat.
"None of us brought our smocks," Smudge pointed out. "Can't you make an exception?"
"You can wear your U-backs, then. But you can't wear those."
"But its freezing!" said Gibbs.
"Look mate, it's on standing orders," said the NCO, clearly getting annoyed. He walked away.
Back at the tent, we got our U-backs which we'd washed the day before and put them on over our softies. We joined the queue again, looking like muscled body builders. No one said anything. Everyone was glued to the X-Factor finals, playing on the flat screen at the far end of the cookhouse. Jedward had just escaped the elimination everyone had looked forward to.

6/11/09 Nad-i-Ali.
In morning we were on QRF again for a 10 liner that never came. The previous night, B coy had gone into Waheed and mopped the floor with the Taliban – 46 killed. Together with our 4, that makes 50 guys not burying IEDs anymore.

8/11/09 Nad-i-Ali.
Another 12 hours sat in a Mastiff guarding a road – 12 hours I'm never going to get back. Thank God nothing happened. Jim was complaining about how there have been hardly any IEDs with us. Nad-i-Ali was supposed to have been a really bad area.
Another thing on tonight's brief- locals in other AO's getting pissed

---

[10] Thick padded jacket

off with TB's IEDs. They putting stones on pressure pads so when the TB connect the batteries....BOOM! Beautiful! Good on 'em! I love those clever chogees.
And MAIL! 3 sacks of mail arrived today. I got loads and loads from the girls and Anna. She sent photos of herself, looking all pretty. I tried calling her back on Saturday but minimise was turned on. Some guy had been shot in the neck on patrol. He'll be okay.

09/11/09. 149 days remaining (?)
Last night I dreamt I was on honeymoon with Anna in some really fancy hotel bit like Crowne Plaza.
Some guy last night on stag was caught in his doss bag. He'd locked the door and didn't wake up even when the orderly officer was kicking it in. He's getting 3 months in Colchester, then dishonourable discharge. Back in the days, he'd be shot for that.

Another QRF/admin day. You take the opportunity to do some admin. Grab a shower once the sun has heated up your solar bag enough. Feels so good to be clean. Also got a lie in this morning, til 8am. Was great! Did some laundry, cos my U-back is now so minging with sweat build up its given me prickly heat. I managed to email once minimise was off, wrote some letters to Anna. And managed to call mom and dad, though mom didn't sound so good. She was wheezing a lot.

My mother had had cancer, which was the other drama going on in my mind aside from getting shot, drowned or blown up. Whenever I had managed to call home on the single phone outside the ops room, I had listened to her voice getting steadily worse and worse.
One day, during a relaxed time in the FOB, someone came by looking for me. I was wanted in the ops room. I instinctively thought I was in trouble. Maybe something I had said on Facebook had been flagged up by the special team of internet censors back at Bastion who spend their tours listening to random phone conversations, and checking emails and Facebook exchanges to make sure secret topics remain secret.
I reported at the ops room, looking sheepish. A captain met me. It wasn't about Facebook. It was about my mother. My father had called the number on the special card that soldiers must give their families. The number was to be called only in a family emergency.

She was in hospital. The doctors assured the army that this was it, and that they had better get me out of Afghanistan to be with her immediately.

In another hour, I was on a helicopter back to Bastion, sitting opposite some American soldiers, looking down at the landscape, where the two sides played cat and mouse with each other. I was enormously glad I would be out of there.

Dave, a giant warrant officer who belonged to another team happened to be at Camp Bastion. He had put himself at my disposal, making sure I had everything I needed for the night journey back to Kuwait, which was where my parents lived. He even brought me a book to read. I couldn't thank him enough.

"Here's my email," he said, giving me a slip of paper. "Make sure you write as soon as things calm down."

It was to be the last time I saw him alive.

From Bastion, an RAF cargo plane flew me to Minadh, an airbase in Dubai. The plane had flown to Afghanistan to drop off two enormous armoured vehicles to replace two others which had been blown up, and the return journey was empty. The crew were kind, and warmed up an Emirates inflight meal which they somehow had managed to procure, while I changed out of my combats into civilian clothing. They let me sit up in the cockpit during landing, wearing the headphones. I listened on the net as a lady in the control tower guided the pilot onto the runway, wondering how my mother was doing since that call. Two RAF personnel dressed in civvies met me off the plane and drove me straight to Dubai International airport. It was one o'clock in the morning.

In the duty-free section, I walked around all the perfume shops and gold stands, wandering aimlessly among tourists. There was no shooting. There were no background radio noises. There were no distant explosions. In the lavatory, the heated toilets flushed themselves and the taps gushed out warm water automatically. At each check out till, there were countless brands of chocolate bars. Families were sitting at McDonalds. The small Filipino women standing behind glass showcases of gold watches were trying to get the attention of over-weight tourists trundling by. It was a very surreal feeling.

My father picked me up from Kuwait airport and together we went straight to the hospital. My mother seemed to have stabilised since he had made that call to the military. She was much better, and very glad to see me back home safely. She chatted away to us both, not making much sense because her brain neurons were beginning to malfunction, happy her son was with her and not fighting some stupid war in some far-off country, happy she was alive, happy I was alive, happy we were all together.

She died early the next morning.

5
Musa Qualeh

107 days remaining

I'm sitting in the RAF plane full of journalists and soldiers returning to Afghanistan from their R and R. One of the journalists is sitting next to me. We'd not really spoken for much of the flight, until the flight attendants began handing out boxes of the evening meal. She took the opportunity to talk to me, though I wasn't in any mood to speak to anyone. No one was, for that matter. The whole cabin had been quiet for the most part of the flight. Some soldiers were reading, but a lot were fast asleep. A few lucky ones had managed to get a whole row of seats to themselves and were lying sideways, legs slightly bent to not stick out into the aisle, arms folded. Conversation between the journalist and I had started with pleasantries typical for passengers on a long flight. I didn't mind that so much.

"So is this the first time you've been to Afghanistan?" she finally asked, in a move away from the small talk. I nodded.

"Will you be staying in Bastion for your tour, or staying in Kandahar?"

"No, not Kandahar," I said. "We're in Helmand. Not Bastion though. We've been mostly in Nad-i-Ali."

"Nad-i-Ali," she said. It seemed like she was trying to locate it on a map in her mind. "That's.."

"It's in the green zone," I said, finishing for her. This was awkward. She looked like she was thinking too much how to pose her next question.

"So, what's it been like?" she asked, cautiously.

I shrugged. "Hot," I said. "It's dusty, and bright. There's flies everywhere." I couldn't really think of anything helpful to say. I didn't really have any real war stories, and even if I had, I don't think I would have opened up, no matter how good looking she was. We'd all been warned about speaking too openly with the media, though I didn't pay much attention because I never really thought I'd get any one-on-one time with a journalist. Now I was sitting next to one, I found my answers were all instinctively guarded. I felt I

should say something more so as not to appear rude.
"You see, I don't really know very much about what's going on because no one ever tells us anything. We just get told what to do each day."
"What is it you do exactly?" she asked.
"Counter-IED."
"Really?" she said, sounding surprised. "Wow." Her eyes had lit up ever so briefly. "You mean, you're the guy who has to defuse the bombs?"
"No, no," I said, stopping her short. "I'm in a search team. We have to find them, then the ATO – that's the bomb guy - he comes and deals with them," I explained. "And it's not just me, there are four of us working together."
She carefully opened the little container of milk, peeling back the lid while mentally building a picture of what I was describing.
"That sounds quite dangerous," she finally said, frowning. We were both trying to stir our tea in ridiculously shallow cups, while trying not to spill it everywhere. No matter how may pots of milk I had put into it, it seemed to vanish and have no effect on the colour.
"Yeah, well…it's dangerous for everyone out on the ground. It doesn't really matter what you do," I said. I didn't really like where this conversation was heading. She was going to tell me how brave she thought I was. I had read about Gordon Brown's announcement to have hundreds of 'specialised troops' trained to deal with the IED threat which was claiming so many casualties. The newspapers described how these soldiers had been specially trained to detect hidden devices. They made it sound so simple. The Taliban changed tactics to IEDs. We trained special troops to find IEDs. The public wanted to know the government had a plan. Problem solved.
"So, who decides what you will be doing when you come out here? Do you volunteer, or do you get told?"
"It's different for different people," I explained. "Depending on the job they need doing. Some would have volunteered to go. I know a few who were ordered to." I smiled. I don't think she understood the organisation she would be embedded with. "This is the Army. You get told what to do. You have to do it."
"Did you volunteer?"
"Yeah."
She paused, studying my face. "You don't really look so keen," she

finally ventured. She was starting to get a bit more genuine in her probing.

"I'm scared," I said quietly so as not to be heard by others.

Another pause. She must not have known what to say to that, so instead she asked, "What made you volunteer for…your job?"

"Well, I had no idea what search was," I admitted, feeling stupid. I exhaled, deciding to elaborate a bit more. "I thought it was searching for…downed pilots or vehicles or something like that. I don't know." I went on. "See, I'd only just got sent to my unit, and they'd all come back from a tour of Afghan, so they were all still drinking from the keg of glory. And there's the new guy who's just tipped up to his unit straight from training, not knowing anything about real soldiering. It's not such a great place to be in, hey," I said, shaking my head.

"I can imagine," she said sympathetically.

"So, one day my troop sergeant calls me into the office and asks if I want to go to Afghan for a search tour. So straight away, I'm like, yeah! Sure!" I rested my head back in the head rest. "Like I said, I wasn't sure what search was. I didn't know what I was getting myself into. I just wanted to go to war." I was fully aware of what an idiot I sounded like.

"Is that what made you join the army?"

"Yes."

"Just not this kind of job."

"No."

There was a pause as she processed everything I had said. Maybe I would read about this stupid conversation in a magazine someday. I hoped not. I would definitely get into trouble.

"Well, I think you're very brave," she said quietly.

I turned to look at her. She must have been in her late twenties. She had long blonde hair rolled up into tight bun, and green eyes. She was very beautiful.

You have no idea, I thought. You have no idea how scared I am. I wanted to tell her. All the time, scared. Brave? If I could somehow figure a way to get us all out of this, trust me I'd take it, in a heartbeat. Why did I volunteer for this? Why? How did I get that stupid?! Brave? It's fine for you to sit there, drinking your tea. You're going to live. In fact, everyone sitting around us, they're all going to live. Everyone is going to live except me. Everyone is going

to come back with war stories to tell their grandkids of how they did their bit in Afghan, except me. Everyone is going to keep their legs except me. But not me. I'm going to make a mistake. I'm going to get blown to bits. I'm going to spend the rest of my life in a wheelchair. Brave? I'm not brave. I'm a coward, you know that? And guess what? I'm not ashamed of it either. I don't care. I just want to live.
But I didn't say any of that. I would have definitely have been in trouble.
"Thanks," I said awkwardly.

The helicopter flight to Musa Qualeh was at dusk. It was at very high altitude and as we flew north, we passed the beginning of the Hindu Kush mountain ranges. We could see them through the small round windows of the Chinook, all highlighted in pink on one side and disappearing in a dusty haze.
The rear ramp of the helicopter was left partially lowered to allow the rear gunner to keep an eye out, and blasts of icy air kept flooding into the interior of the machine. On each side of me, soldiers sat strapped into the seat rack, hands resting on the butts of their upturned rifles and waiting patiently to land again. The man beside me turned and shouted something in my ear, but it was a few attempts before I understood what he was trying to say.
"Tell the gunner to close the door!" he joked. I smiled and huddled deeper into my body armour, trying not to expose any skin.
After about twenty minutes, the helicopter suddenly made a nose dive, causing everyone's stomachs to lurch. People were muttering under their breath and shaking their heads at the pilot's wild flying. As far as I was aware, helicopter pilots always flew very high when making longer journeys to avoid getting shot down. Then when they were in the area they would descend very rapidly like a screaming eagle, while the escorting Apache kept a watch from above.
The Chinook was quickly losing height, causing our ears to pop, and then suddenly we were on a roller coaster ride, only none of us could see where we were heading. The Chinook was hugging the ground and flying very fast, going up slopes, and then suddenly down the opposite side. More lurches, more swearing, then a hard left, then banking right. Out of the rear ramp occasionally I could catch glimpses ploughed fields below us as we shot past. We were very

low. Beads of sweat are trickling down my forehead despite the cold, and I'm beginning to want to vomit. The man besides me had his eyes closed and looked pale.
Without warning, the Chinook flared. Our world suddenly sloped upwards as the helicopter lost all its speed and made a quick, gentle landing on the HLS.
The usual line of soldiers was crouched by the perimeter, helmets down and looking in the other direction as the initial blast of down draft swept over them. Then the disembarkation process began. The new soldiers ran off, formed a chain and began offloading the mountain of kit, while the old soldiers adjusted their loads into ways in which they could move quickly, and waited for the loadmaster's signal.
In another minute the Chinook was airborne again, and disappeared over the walls as fast as possible, taking with it the link to the outside world. The noise level dropped immediately.

While I was away at my mother's funeral, everyone else had been whisked away to Musa Qualeh, a desert, hilly region further up in the north of Helmand. They were all waiting for me at the HLS as the chopper flew off, smiling and hugging me and giving me a hand with all my kit. I was glad they were around.
Later on, after I had dumped my kit off at the tent we were billeted, Gibbs gave me a tour around camp, telling me all the latest. The search team had had their first finds. Gibbs had found three devices, and Lee had found a battery pack off to the side of the road. Gibbs also had another lucky escape. They were searching a road, when he had stepped on a pressure plate, right in line with an alleyway. I stopped walking when I heard that.
"I was shitting it," he said. "I didn't know what to do."
"Why didn't it go off?"
"The battery was dead."
The old fear came flooding back. A dead battery. That was all that had prevented the worst thing that can happen to a search team. A week before, another team had been blown up. Their ATO had lost both his legs, and the team commander was dead. The squadron had lost its first man in the first few weeks of our tour. Someone from the ops room came to pack up his kit to get sent home. He had also

been killed by an IED.
“I suppose you’re counting that as a find,” I said.

That night, a comedian who had come on the same helicopter as me gave a comedy performance in the cookhouse tent filled with soldiers. He was very funny, and made the crowd roar with laughter. I was in the front row between the two Steve’s, feeling the muzzle of my rifle, smiling at each joke. They were good. I couldn’t stop missing my mother.
Outside, the overcast clouds which had blocked out the bright Afghan stars rumbled with thunder, drowning out the din of soldiers coming from the canvas tent.

Musa Qualeh had once been a Taliban stronghold until the fighting of the previous years in which the town had changed hands a couple of times. At the time we arrived, the area was more or less firmly ours and had become an important supply depot for the surrounding region. There was another large base not far away on the other side of a wadi called FOB Edinburgh and there was artillery emplaced there. A road linked the two bases, and it stretched all the way back to Camp Bastion. Enormous convoys manned by the RLC would leave Bastion and make their periodic journeys up north to Musa Qualeh with all types of supplies the Army needed to fight a war. These journeys were long and dangerous. Sometimes trucks would be blown up by IEDs or ambushed, but generally the roads were being kept open. Ammunition, medical supplies, toilet paper, replacement vehicles and spare parts, fresh food and fuel would all be organised into iso-containers by the quarter-master. From Musa Qualeh, supplies would be reorganised and sent onto the various network of small outposts dotted around the countryside. These patrol bases were designed to keep the roads open, and from them infantry patrols would leave each night looking for Taliban to kill.

One Taliban group in the area had recently defected from the insurgency and, with the co-operation of the Afghan National Police, had set up a militia in their home village. That night, we gathered in sheltered area between the two tents we had been billeted in and Troopie gave us all the details of the next day’s operation. A large makeshift table sat in the middle of the passage way, surrounded by improvised benches made of logs, wire and old mouldy blankets. Everything smelt of damp. The table itself, normally covered with crossword puzzles, candle wax and old board games now had the aerial map on which Troopie was regurgitating all the details he had jotted down during the O Group. The map itself was illuminated by half a dozen head torches facing down as everyone listened to the details of the latest operation we had to go on. Beyond this circle of torch-light was immediate thick darkness.

"The place is called Shar Khariz. It's..." - he stopped his speech, struggling to locate the particular group of hamlets - "over there somewhere, about a couple of hours drive but I expect it will take a lot longer to get there. A militia group of ex-Taliban fighters have all defected over to ISAF, and the commanders here want to get in contact with them. So, we'll be tagging along as QRF to any possible IED explosions." He paused to go over his notes in the light of his head torch.

So far, so good. As Quick Reaction Force, we would only be called into action if one of the vehicles hit an IED. That meant there was a chance, if nothing happened, that we would not have to do any searching at all.

"Er, ah yes, there's also a compound not too far away where they want to park one of the Mastiffs in a stag position facing the FLET." My heart sank. He continued.

"So obviously they would like it searched before they park up." He paused, looking around at all the faces sitting round the table. It was raining outside, and pitch black. The rain was being blown in from the side and gradually soaking the soldiers at the edge of overhead shelter. "Any questions?"

"Why did they defect?" someone asked from the darkness.

"What was that Sapper Gibbs?"

"The militia," said Gibbs. "How come they defected over to our side?"

"Ah yeah," said Troopie, supressing a smirk. "The Taliban were forbidding them to use their mobile phones because they know we can intercept them. So, they got fed up of that and came over to our side."

The convoy of Mastiffs left the next day at dawn. We had been told to expect to be out on the ground for up to three days, so the night before, rations, water and the all-important wag bags had been distributed to everyone. The infantry had been up before dawn, warming up the vehicles and checking radio communications. There was no space for everyone's bergens inside the vehicles, so instead they were hung by carabiners off the bar armour on the side where they swung violently to and fro with every pothole and rut. We were driving off road wherever we could, each Mastiff was zigzagging in its own random path, like a fleet of ships on a heaving sea. Inside each vehicle, despite being tightly strapped in, bodies were being thrown around. Soft tissue was being jarred against hard surfaces. Although the convoy was not travelling very fast, it was enough to throw objects and people up into the air when a vehicle hit a sudden dip, sending a chorus of swear words up to the driver.
I nudged my helmet forward slightly, over my eyes and tried to sleep. I was car-sick. I needed fresh air. I needed to get out, take this body armour off, arch my back and straighten my legs before getting into a hot bath and falling asleep. My headache throbbed in time with my heart beat and there's a bad stale taste in my mouth. My breath probably smells, I thought. Where's my gum? My mind functions sluggishly. All I could think of is the smell of fumes and body odour. Did I bring any? Nausea. Mouth fills with saliva. Smudge yelling at the driver. The massive engine revving below us. Map pockets. Check map pockets. My fingers slowly take the gloves off of one hand, which then stretches out in weak feeble attempts at the pocket at my thigh, straining against the shoulder straps which have tightly fastened my body into the seat. My leg tries freeing itself for a second before I get a moment of clarity: Give Up. Exertion. Throbbing. Stop. Leave It. Just Be Calm.

After two hours, which seemed to never end, we suddenly seemed to be manoeuvring. The other passengers had long since abandoned their angry protests at the driver and had simply sat in silence, facing each other patiently waiting for the end. We only realised we had reached our destination when we sensed we were reversing. The gunner was giving directions down to the driver on their head-sets they both wore, and then crouched down.

"We're here," he said.
As the two doors swung open, sunlight and fresh air poured into the inside of the vehicle, and everyone began the clumsy clamber out, one by one. For the first time, we could see where we were. We had driven into the middle of a large walled enclosure. There was only one big two storey building, looking either half-finished or half destroyed. Like a house of cards, it looked like it would collapse at any minute. Metal rebar sprouted out of concrete pillars, waiting to impale anything that should happen to fall onto it. Here and there were makeshift shelters of plastic, or ragged cloth walls flapping in the wind.
The three Mastiffs up ahead of us which had arrived first had emptied all the troops they carried and were now parked in the centre of the open space in a defensive cruciform, with the rear of each vehicle facing each other, and the front facing outwards in a triangle. A couple of other soldiers had launched a toy plane for aerial reconnaissance, while the officers went over to greet the leader of the Shar-Khariz militia accompanied by their tangeeman.
Our little group watched all these developments from where we had clustered together beside our Mastiff. So far, we had managed to stay invisible to everyone, and were lying in the sun amongst a sea of equipment we had with us, recovering from the journey. I began hoping that the planned search had been forgotten about. Although we were at Shar-Khariz to officially welcome the militia to ISAF and find out a bit more about them, we didn't trust them for a second. One of the first things we discovered about our new allies was one of their casualties they had suffered the day before we arrived. According to them, their former Taliban comrades in the area had attacked the compound we were now sun bathing in with up to a hundred men, though of course the militia had heroically beaten off the attack with great determination and skill. Our medic went over to examine the body of the man who had been killed the previous day and came back with some worrying news.
"He's been strangled," he announced. "Murdered, by one of these lot," he said, glancing at the group of men sitting on the concrete roof of the building. "Someone obviously didn't like him."
We all discreetly studied them without making our fascination too obvious. There were more inside the dark confines of the building, lounging around and completely uninterested in the arrival of the

British Army to their hide out. There was one bearded individual on the roof clad in black, talking with the rest of his small group. So, there they were. Real live Taliban. Or, to be more precise, real live *former* Taliban. Now they were known as the Shar-Khariz Militia. Below in the compound, a few members of the Afghan police had shown up, shouldering their collapsible AK-47s as they got out of the Toyota. The ex-Taliban seemed much more interested in them and the two groups greeted each other in their tradition and began a conversation in Pashtun. Eventually one of the roof-dwellers came down and joined the policemen at the car, who had by now opened the bonnet and were examining the engine. Everything seemed innocent and normal, apart from the fact that a murder-victim was right there in the presence of the ANP. Life is cheap. No one cared.

"So they murder their own people, and the only reason why they're on our side is because they're not allowed to use their phones," said Lee, bemused. "Great! I'm sleeping in the middle tonight."

"So, what, are they're sulking or something?" asked Gibbs, smiling in disbelief. "I don't believe this."

"I don't want any of you lot wandering off by yourselves," said Smudge authoratively. "And no one is taking their body armour off either."

The planned search later that day was not forgotten about. Soon we were led to a nearby compound where one of the Mastiffs would be parked for the night to keep an eye out for enemy. We were all detailed off in various areas to check the ground for hidden booby traps before the infantry could go in, though after two hours nothing was found. During that search, one of those small miracles that happen from time to time in one's life happened to me.

The search was nearly over. I was working my way slowly up to a doorway, with Smudge following some distance behind me, stepping in my footprints. To our left, the scenery is breath-taking. The Musa Qualeh area is much higher up than further south in the green zone. The landscape is brown and rugged, constantly rising and falling with waves of wadis and mountain ridges. I had already taken half a dozen photos of the mountains that day, but as usual when trying to capture such scenery, the picture pales in comparison.

We gradually closed in on the doorway. Smudge was keeping an eye out for me, constantly scanning the distance with his telescopic sights, as I gave the ground most of my attention. I was just checking the ground at the door way itself when Smudge asked if I had my trip wire feeler –a length of metal wire every searcher keeps on them to detect trip wires in doorways – and I had just replied yes, before looking down and silently panicking as I realised it was gone, when suddenly the Vallon gave off a high shriek, right in the middle of the gap. A classic place IED's are buried. I turned to Smudge.

"I think this might be something."

"Cool, I'll let you crack on," he said, backing away a safe distance.

I made sure he was lying prone before kneeling down to check what the Vallon had detected. Very slowly, I brushed away the earth, expecting to reveal a corner of a pressure plate. Instead, I found a small piece of metal wire. It was the right length, and thinner than the wire I normally carried. The perfect trip wire feeler, just when I needed it, just when I was about to get into trouble for not having one. I couldn't believe it.

"It's nothing," I said to Smudge, getting up on my knees.

"Okay mate. Make sure you check the doorway for trip wires too."

After that, Smudge and I returned to the main group, just as the gunner gave a shout.

"Stand to! Stand to!" he cried, pointing in the direction of the FLET. Several men stood a few hundred metres away in a small cluster, not moving. Just standing there watching us. We had initially taken cover, expecting an RPG to come hurtling towards us. How long had they been there? Are they enemy? Every one of us had our weapons trained on them, looking at the group of men through our telescopic sights. They made no move.

The trouble with fighting a guerrilla war is that you never knew who the enemy are, while all the time they know who you are. The army had issued a new policy called Courageous Restraint, which meant that soldiers first had to identify someone as an enemy before opening fire. You can't just shoot anything that moves. You had to see them with a weapon, and even then, you could not be certain because a lot of Afghans kept weapons anyway. Before our deployment to the war, we had been given lectures on the Laws of Armed Combat, and the Rules of Engagement adopted by the British army. We had been told of scenarios in the past in Iraq where both British and American soldiers had been too trigger-happy, or too nervous and ended up killing civilians by mistake. The whole point of Courageous Restraint, we were told, was to get the locals on our side, and not shooting up their family would go a long way in making us seem like the right side to be on.

The negative aspect of this policy was being played out at that moment for soldiers on the ground. The group of men were surely Taliban. Who else could they be? They were in the direction of known enemy. There were no women or children. On the other hand, none of them had any weapons we could see. Maybe they weren't Taliban.

The silence was broken by Troopie.

"Well," he said, lowering his rifle. "We're not achieving anything by standing here. Let's head back to the building. We've done our job."

We left the small group of infantry with their Mastiff to make themselves as comfortable as possible for the coming night in the area we had searched for them. The gunner kept his heavy machine gun trained on the distant audience as they watched us depart.

That night the wind kept waking me up. We had all bedded down between the main wall and another parked Mastiff, sleeping side by side on the stony ground. Although the cloudless day had been fairly warm and pleasant, the heat disappeared as soon as the sun had set behind the mountains. It was a bitterly cold night. In the early evening, a brief exchange of machine gun fire in the direction of the Mastiff came in over the high walls we lay behind.

"I guess they were Taliban after all," remarked one of the soldiers in the IEDD team.

A few of us joked with those sleeping on the edges about getting kidnapped during the night by the militia and subjected to scenes from the film *Hostel*. Hopefully, the Taliban wouldn't text their former friends: YOU'RE ALLOWED TO USE YOUR PHONES IF YOU KILL THEM ALL IN THEIR SLEEP LOL XX.

Well before dawn, we were quietly woken up for Stand-To. The ground was hard and rocky and stones had been digging into my body all night. Beside me, a soldier with an incredibly lined face was packing his doss bag into his bergen. Shadowy figures all around are quietly getting their boots on while still in their doss bags before finally braving the cold and getting completely out and stuffing it

away. Before I had gone to bed, I had changed out of my dirty, sweaty U-back and put on my pyjama top – a t-shirt set aside for the soul purpose of sleeping in. Now as I fumbled around in the darkness to find the day-time U-back, I realised I had made a crucial mistake and left it out of the doss bag the night before, and not had it inside with me to keep it warm. When I finally found it, it was icy cold and made me take a sharp intake of breath as I put it on.
We stood around in our body armour and helmets during Stand To for about an hour. Push ups helped keep warm. Gradually the sky lightened into grey dawn, and the stars started disappearing. When it was light enough, Stand To was announced to be over by the ATO in charge of the IEDD team. He was a captain in the RLC.
"Don't think you're getting back into bed," he told a couple of men who had made a move to get their sleeping bags out again. "Let's get some breakfast on the go."

As the sun rose, we found out what we would be waiting for that day. A *Shura* had been called that morning, for all the village elders to come to discuss important issues with the commanders. No one really told us what exactly was to be talked about, and once again, none of us cared a great deal. It seemed as though we would be heading back to the base when the meeting was over, so the sooner it began, the better. In the meantime, we stayed armed and ready, cooking our breakfasts over small fires and boiling water for ration-sachets of disgusting, burnt-tasting army coffee. Nothing happened. Gibbs, both Steve's, Lee and I sat on the ground, enjoying the warmth of the sun. Smudge came over to join us, laying his rifle down on the ground by his feet.
"What are we talking about?" he asked.
"Oh, we're all just planning Gibbs's life for him," I joked. "He's signing off."
"I'm signing off" confirmed Gibbs. "This is shit. Searching is shit. All we do is rummage around in the sand looking for bombs."
"Not what you thought it would be, is it?" mused Smudge, lighting a cigarette.
"Any ideas?" someone asked. "What trade are you?" Everyone in the Royal Engineers was supposed to be taught a certain trade, though few people were ever lucky enough to actually get experience once they were sent to their units.

"BNSF," he said. A plasterer.
"There's good money in Crete for that," I chimed in. "Ex-pats there are always looking for an English speaking handy-man to work on their holiday houses. You could go over there, work on people's holiday homes all winter when they're away and live it up in the summer. Find yourself a Greek girl. Actually practise your trade for once."
"Crete?" he said, looking not so sure. "I was thinking about North Sea oil rigs. That's good money, that. Was thinking about working on one of them for a couple of years."
"Better money than what we're bringing back," Lee remarked bitterly. Soldiers got about two thousand four hundred pounds bonus at the end of a six-month tour, in addition to their monthly salaries. Each man's wages would be different, depending on how long you had served in the military. In addition, soldiers could claim a small amount of money for each day spent away from home. Again, this depended on how many days you had accumulated throughout your career. For new soldiers like us, six months amounted to just over a thousand pounds. Each of us had long since calculated how much money we would save at the end of six months, if we managed to come back alive. Together with claims, bonuses and regular wages, I should have just over ten thousand pounds waiting for me. Searchers were still not receiving any danger pay like the ATOs, which was a source of bitter contention everyone had with the army. Both jobs were extremely dangerous, but many of us would rather walk down a road to deal with a hidden device which had already been discovered, rather than walk down a road and have to find them before you step on one.
"You don't want to go with North Sea oil, Gibbs," I said. "It'll just be another thing you do with your life for a couple of years before you move onto the next thing. You need to stick with your trade while you're still young." Gibbs had spent his birthday while we were in Shawquat. His family had sent him out a small foot-ball cake which he shared with us in the tent one night. He had just turned twenty. "Besides, the North Sea sounds freezing. Crete's much better."
"Bobby's right," Smudge said. "Work on your trade as much as possible when you get out."
A love-hate relationship had developed between Smudge and Gibbs.

The young soldier and old soldier were constantly annoying each other, because it seemed to me that Smudge had taken on an almost paternal role when it came to Gibbs. He had been in the army for about twenty years. Our Troopie, who was waiting with the other officers for the shura to begin, was the only other member of the team who had been to Afghan before, and that was only for a little while.

Little Steve and Gibbs, who had been friends before, had been making plans for their post tour leave to go to America for a few weeks when this was all over. They had become the married couple in the team, and were a search pair. Some tasks only required two men, and within a team, the four searchers naturally fell into unofficial pairs. Lee and I were the other search pair. I had mixed feelings about Lee. He was well natured, not the malicious type. But I couldn't understand what he was doing in the army, or how he had managed to pass the training in the first place. Back in our unit in the UK, there always seemed to be something wrong with various parts of his body which would excuse him from squadron PT. But he still had a find, when I hadn't. The IED scores were: Gibbs, four and Lee, one. That left Little Steve and I at the bottom with a frustrating zero. The fact that neither of us had found any IEDs yet left us both feeling emasculated as searchers. We knew searchers in other teams had by now found loads more. The current record was held by a Gurkha in another team. He had just found his seventeenth. "Look, lads," Smudge would say to console us. "You can't find what ain't there. Don't worry about it. You've not missed anything, as long as we all get back okay, I couldn't care." He looked at us. "*Do* you care? *Really*?"

"No," we both said glumly.

The whole of that morning lying in the sun, planning Gibbs's future, not knowing if the former Taliban a stone's throw away could be trusted or not, remain in my mind as a fond memory. Later on, towards eleven or twelve, Afghan men began showing up from the surrounding countryside for the shura. They were all older men, over fifty, and most of them wore white traditional robes, indicating that they held places of esteem in their society. I had learnt that from our tangeeman. White meant he was at the top. Any other colour meant a lower class, though I could never remember which colour robe out ranked which other colour.

A great crowd gathered in a large semi-circle by the cruciform of Mastiffs, with a group of officers sitting facing them, accompanied by a translator. They spoke for a long time, discussing matters which were well beyond the interest of bored soldiers sitting behind machine guns and grenade launchers, scanning their arcs and sipping hot brews from their thermos flasks, while holding shuras of their own. Discussing women, and leave, and a life after the army.

Much later in the afternoon, the convoy started its engines. The commanders made sure they shook hands with the tribal leader, the militia leader, the tribal leader's tribal followers, the militia leader's militia cohorts, the Afghan Policemen and the leader of the group of Little Mischievous Boys who had been spying on the shura, as Little Mischievous Boys do when grownups discuss grownup things. Even the tangeeman could not escape the hand shaking frenzy he suddenly found himself in, as the officers made sure every Afghan hand was diligently shaken. A few were even caught shaking each other's hands on a job well done.
"Jolly good show, Darling!"
"Oh, bravo Sir!"
"I daresay, Darling, the men look rather bored with nothing to do. Can't have that in the ranks! No sir!"
"No Sir! Not good for morale, Sir."
"Sergeant Major!"
"*SARRRR*!"
"Time to show these Little Mischievous Boys what British soldiers are made of!"
"Tis indeed Sarrr! I know just the thing Sarrr!"
"And what would that be, Sergeant Major?"
"*SIDEBURNS PARADE, SARRR!*"
"Bravo!"
"Oh, Capitol!"
"Carry on, Sergeant Major!"
The only Afghan whose hand didn't get shaken was the dead man. But no one wanted to bring that one up. We didn't want to annoy our new friends.

Minden is a Patrol Base, not far away from the main base in Musa Qualeh. The helicopter dropped us off with all our equipment, and left us with the waiting infantry who had sallied out of the walls of the compound to form a perimeter around the landing site. The Sea King had also dropped off a small mound of supplies, and each man crammed as many water bottles and cans of food as he could carry and ran towards the entrance before running out for more.

The small garrison of infantry had been responsible for the stretch of road running through the area, which was inhabited by civilians. I can't remember the name of the village, but my journal shows that we were dropped off there just a few days before Christmas. The infantry platoon had no place for us to stay except a tent in which they had miraculously set up a flat screen TV. Throughout our stay there, it showed repeats of Christmas pop music. It did nothing but make everyone homesick and remind us that we're spending Christmas sleeping on the floor of an icy tent.

The commander of the garrison had a few main objectives his men wanted to use but they suspected the Taliban had buried IED's in all of them. One was a bridge, one was a crossing point which led down into a main wadi, and the last was a firing point on top of a hill which both the infantry and the Taliban had been using because from it you could hit targets for a long way in every direction.
There was also an IED which had been discovered the previous day by a foot patrol along a track leading into the village, and everyone wanted it taken care of. The locals living there co-exist with IED's. They have to learn where to walk, and read the subtle warning signs that the Taliban leave out for them. These could be a small line of stones, or a piece of shredded plastic that's been tied around a tree or hanging from a branch. The kind of every day thing that a foreigner won't notice, or might notice, think a bit odd, and then think nothing more of.

That evening, we set out on patrol with the escorting soldiers towards the village, walking up a slope along the road. After about twenty minutes we broke onto a track. The commander of the infantry was speaking to our Troopie, motioning that the device was just up ahead. Everyone dumped their kit as soon as it became apparent that this was the closest we were going. For the three of us carrying the heavy ECM, the question going through our minds all the time when going on patrol is, when can I stop and take the weight off my back? Even that short twenty-minute hike was beginning to burn my shoulders. Little Steve and Lee had been up ahead and had searched an area where we could sit down. Now they were further up with the ATO, clearing an area closer to the device for him to work from. For the rest of us, it was a matter of waiting and keeping an eye open for any enemy. No one was expecting anything though. It was a peaceful evening. The sun was slowly nearing the horizon and cast a reddish-brown shade to the surrounding landscape, and the shadows of the buildings were creeping up the hills like the fingers of a gloved hand. Some of the locals, who had been waiting for the IED to finally be removed, had come to watch the explosion from a distance. We had to wave them away and signal with our hands that there was going to be a blast, and they nodded and herded their children away.

The ATO returned from working on the IED. “It’s a big cooking pot,” he said. “About twenty-five kilos, so there’s going to be a pretty big bang”.

Cooking pots were not the best choice to make an IED out of, because they gave off a very high reading with a metal detector. It would have been so easy to find it.

This information got passed down the line, and digital cameras came out and set to film it as the ATO went back again to set his final charge. Twenty-five kilograms would be a really big bang. I tried following where exactly along the ridge the bomb was supposed to be. There was no wind. Everything looked so calm and innocent.

The ATO was walking back with another man to a safe distance, and yelled back “One minute!”

That got passed down the line again to the men protecting the rear. “There’s going to be a controlled explosion in one minute,” everyone was saying.

I’m still looking at the general area where the ATO had been working, curious where it had been buried. The camera held up high, still rolling.

The ATO turned back to us with his hands cupped and yelled “Firing! FIRING NOW!”

The ridge line erupts like a volcano, shooting a column of reddish-brown earth high into the air. The thunderclap echoed off the hills and travelled down the valley. That would have scattered the man standing on it, and sent the two men either side of him to the hospital at Bastion. Everyone started laughing, and giving low whistles, watching the pillar of dust slowly drift away. A ring had formed right at the top of the dust cloud and floated toward the village. "That was a bloody short one minute" some Irishman joked, and everyone laughed again. That was a big explosion, and no one was hurt. We were just relieved.

PB Minden was a cold place to be at night. It was small enough as it was with the handful of infantry that garrisoned it. These patrol bases were like dots in a sea of unsearched ground. That's how a searcher mentally categorises ground in Afghan. Not 'ours' and 'theirs', or 'friendly' and 'hostile', or even 'road' and 'field'. It's always either searched ground, or unsearched ground. I had only been in the country three months and the idea of walking off into an unsearched area was like being told to play Russian roulette.
The stag points where the sentries took turns at watching the road running past the walls could see all the way up to where there was a bend in the distance. A few days before we arrived, someone had seen two men digging in the road just before the bend. One had been kneeling with a rifle, keeping watch while the other man behind him was attacking the ground with a shovel. The commander had been able to film all this with night vision, and then after he had gathered enough information he needed, he ordered the sniper beside him to kill them. The sniper's first shot hit the man digging full in the chest, and he went sprawling backwards and immediately lay still. The second man must not have heard anything at first because he carried on keeping a look out. Only when he turned and saw his dead friend did he suddenly react, and it saved his life. He dived round the corner before the sniper let off another round. The commander was going to send out a patrol to recover the body, but a while later the second man came back with a group of children. He used them to screen himself while the children began to drag the body back behind the corner.

I went to bed that night, lying deep at the bottom of my sleeping bag in the foetal position. I could not stop shaking and both my hands were clenched in fists between my thighs. Troopie had told us about the bridge that lay just beyond the bend in the road which no one

could see. The blind spot where Taliban had been seen digging. The infantry wanted to use the bridge on the other side so that they could send the Warriors around that way to flank a known Taliban stronghold. A Warrior which had tried crossing off road had been blown up, and the commander had requested a search team to open up the roads so he had more options with which to attack the Taliban. Beyond the bridge, there was a hill. It guarded one approach to the village which the Taliban were occupying and was so heavily booby-trapped that the infantry dubbed it "IED Hill". They had stopped trying to go up it, but instead waited until we arrived.
Once again, I couldn't sleep. I couldn't stop conjuring up the road, the bend, the bridge, and the hill. I was cold, and scared. Sometime towards midnight, I stopped shivering and fell asleep.

The patrol was lined up in marching order shortly after daybreak. The sun had not really gained any height yet, and it was still bitterly cold. Misty breath appeared all along the line of soldiers who stood around in a loose line. Each man was slightly doubled over with a small mountain on his back. The signaller was checking the radio communication, and some Warriors had been driven up to the patrol base. The engines were idling outside in a rhythmic *chug-chug-chug-chug-chug-chug-chug*. Smudge was there in front of me, patiently waiting for the order to go. As usual, he had the heaviest ECM.
I don't remember much of the patrol out, except there was a brief contact further up. A burst of shooting sent everyone down on the ground, facing outwards. Troopie and Lee had taken cover behind the halted Warrior and were lying prone on the ground, looking up with inquisitive looks on their faces. Taking cover with ECM on your back is always awkward. Not only is it uncomfortable and impossible to shoot straight when prone, but you also need to roll over to take it off and then sit it upright so the antenna stays pointing up. But there was no more shooting, and after a few minutes the patrol was moving on again. None of us really knew what the shooting had been about. What I did know was that I was cold and wanted to get back in my sleeping bag. Getting shot at in the first few minutes of the day was becoming more of an annoyance, especially when you're forced to lie on frozen ground and can't see anyone to shoot back.
We arrived at the bend where the line of sight to the patrol base

disappeared. We could see in the background the low walls where we had exited two hours earlier. It didn't seem so far away at all. A Warrior had stayed with us as we began our search for protection, while infantry on either side took up positions to keep an eye on us. They had had to search their own ground to get to these firing positions. On each side some poor man had been chosen to search ahead of each patrol, but they had been able to choose a path at random, and that was enormous protection.

We began like any other search. Being left-handed, I was on the left shoulder of the road. It meant I could swing the Vallon a little bit further away from the road and find any batteries that had been buried off to the side. Then Little Steve did the same on the right. Behind us was Gibbs and Lee. Each man kept a certain distance from each other, and behind us all was Smudge who was co-ordinating everyone.

The four searchers move at a very slow pace. Each time someone shouts out "check on", everyone stops, takes a knee and waits while that man has a careful dig around to investigate any suspicious readings his metal detector has given. You could be kneeling for five or ten minutes. During our training, we had been taught to lie down each time someone would confirm something by digging around with their hands, but we quickly realised how tiring this was. Some roads had so much metal embedded in them that literally each step one of the four of us would shout "check on", and have to wait until everyone was lying prone before he could proceed to rummage through the ground. Every nut and bolt and tin can would have to be dug up, thrown off to the side and then the hole had to be checked again to make sure the metal wasn't just a decoy. Sometimes the Taliban would do that. They would bury an IED and then scatter metallic objects all over the area, hoping that a searcher would eventually get so frustrated that he will assume the next time the Vallon makes a noise it will be just another bit of scrap metal. Or, sometimes there won't be any IED at all. They will just scatter metal along the road anyway. It's enough to slow down any kind of movement along a road for hours.

The ground on that road was very, very hard. It was full of rocks and small stones and there were puddles of icy water. Thick undergrowth bordered each side, and piles of rubbish was littered everywhere. It

all had to be thoroughly searched.
It took us about three hours to cover the fifty meters of the bend which the Cortez camera back at the patrol base could not see. The surveillance camera sits on a mast and can be pivoted in any direction. It had produced the video footage of the IED team that had been caught trying to dig in a device along the road we were on, and which members of the Intelligence Corps back at Bastion were probably busy studying over cups of coffee at that moment.
Just before we got to the bridge, I came across an object that caught my eye deep in the long grass. It was sticking out of the ground and looked like some sort of plunger. I froze.
"Check on!" I shouted to the others. We all knelt down, them waiting patiently to get going again, while I took a closer look at whatever this was, carefully brushing the grass aside. I swept the Vallon over it, and it gave a high shriek. There it was, sticking out of the ground. It looked like a small plunger, going into a cylinder. Was it an MUV switch? I had never seen one before. Reluctantly, I got down prone and signalled the others to do so too. They all took cover and waited. I had been carefully digging around for a while now but was not finding where the metal tone was coming from, so I stopped and had a good look at the object, too afraid to touch it. What was this thing? Is it going to explode?
After a few minutes, Smudge called out from behind me "what do you see, buddy?"
"I don't know" I yelled back. "It's white, and sticks directly out of the ground. It looks like something you're supposed to tread on."
"It's up to you mate." The ATO was beside him, ready come forward. I decided I'd done my bit.
"Find!" I shouted back. That was the signal for the others to get up off the ground and head back one by one, while I marked out on the ground for the ATO to find before getting up and walking back to the others. I described exactly what I had seen, and off Doug went to confirm if it was a bomb. A tremendous relief was taken off my shoulders now that someone else was taking over. If it was an IED, then it was over to him. Lee, Gibbs Steve and I spent five minutes at the rear speculating what it could be, occasionally taking a glance over at Doug to see how he was getting along. He was crouched over the same patch of earth I had been, and digging into the soil with a bayonet until he came back with the unearthed object in his hand. It

was a used syringe with the needle still on the end. The plunger I had seen sticking suspiciously out of the ground had been the part that gets pushed with the thumb and it happened to be half buried and standing straight up. A syringe covered over with grass, giving off a high metal tone and in an area where two men had been seen digging a few nights before had been the latest reason to make me nervous of everything in Afghanistan.
"Well," said the ATO with a smile. "At least you found it. Shows you're doing your job."

It was the first of many needles I found that day. It seemed Afghanistan had a serious drug problem, and the discarded needles lying around everywhere was another problem to soldiers when they were getting ambushed and diving for cover. You had to be careful where you dived, not just because you might dive onto a bomb, but you might also impale yourself on someone else's used needle. We had been warned about needles when we first got to Afghanistan. One soldier had dived into some cover during a contact only to feel a sharp burning sensation in his hip. Thinking he had been shot, he looked down only to see a syringe protruding from his abdomen. The bridge we had been heading to was evidently a gathering place of local drug users. There were needles everywhere. Steve and I searched under the bridge to make sure there were no bombs fixed to the underside, then slowly searched through the mud underneath. It smelt of human faeces and was littered with used syringes. It was grim. From the other side I could hear Steve swearing under his breath. We both stopped and looked at each other.
"This is shit," he said.
"Yup," I said, standing straight to stretch my back. "There's no way I'm diving into this, man."
Behind him in the river bed was the enormous crater which had blown up the Warrior which had tried to cross off-road. It was full of water, and Gibbs was busy searching the edges of it for secondary devices. The Warrior which had been assigned to protect us had been creeping forward all morning as we slowly progressed up to the bridge and now Lee was searching an area off the track for the vehicle to manoeuvre. Usually, the infantry signaller carrying the radio would listen to the net for i-com chatter. When the Taliban talk to each other over the radio, our interpreters could listen in with their

hand-held radio sets that they carried with them. They would then translate everything that was being said, and the signaller would pass it on over the net so that everyone involved with an operation would know what the Taliban were saying to each other. Often it would be a running commentary on our movements. Today though, i-com chatter had been quiet. In fact, thankfully, it was another quiet day. Later on, we were told we were forgetting about searching up IED Hill. There was a graveyard up most of it and the areas where there weren't graves were so channelled that it would be hardly any room for a Warrior to manoeuvre around on the ridge. They would only be at risk of getting hit by an RPG from the village just beyond. It was up to the commanders to determine a different way of getting at the village, but for us it meant the searching for the day was over.

We are standing, all holding the body bag with a corpse inside. It's zipped up, but the man inside is not dead. He's thrashing around, trying to get out. But none of us holding the six handles react. We're all quiet, looking in the same direction as the Chinook lands on the HLS. Slowly, we jostle forward as though in a ceremony and load the screaming bag onto the ramp.
I wake up, shivering with cold and glad it's only a nightmare.

That morning, we were up at dawn again to head off in the direction of the wadi where the infantry wanted a route cleared for their Warriors to get down into the riverbed. It was going to be a bit different this time. The Taliban force in the area were well aware by now of our presence and overnight they had been talking about us on their radios. The only other i-comm chatter we had heard was when the Sea King had dropped us off at Minden. One of the Taliban had asked a single question: "Are you able to shoot down the helicopter?" But the chopper pilots were too fast, darting across the landscape like dragonflies.
For the past couple of days though, there had been very little talk from the Taliban, until we had arrived at the wadi. Across the dried up river, somewhere on the opposite bank was a Taliban position. The infantry, who had taken up their positions facing the other side kept scanning the distant tree line for any sign of movement. So did everyone in our team. I was crouching beside Lee, staring hard

through my sights, slowly creeping the aiming needle along the bank.
Only five minutes ago one of our tangeemen had announced the bit of information he had intercepted on the Taliban radio frequencies. "Bring up the PKMs". Machine guns. No one could see anything.
It was still early morning, and the infantry commander, who wanted to achieve this objective before lunch, was eager to get going.
"We've got you covered," he was saying. "When the shooting starts, just sprint back here. Don't worry, we got more firepower than they have," he said, turning to the two Warriors behind us. They had both traversed their gun turrets to bring their canons to bear out across the wadi.
Slowly, cautiously, we searched our way down the beaten track. I tried concentrating on what I was doing, but as we made our way past the line of infantry lying prone behind their machine guns, I was painfully aware that it was only us that were standing up. We were walking towards the edge of the track where it descended down into the riverbed, but no one could see yet how steep the cliff was. The Taliban had said to bring up their machine guns, but where were they? Why weren't they firing yet? How many guns did they have? Was there a sniper? Were they waiting for us to get further away from the Warriors? Were they aiming at me? How long would it take a round to travel the distance? I judged about a second.
After ten minutes, there was still no shooting, and no IEDs. The silence was deafening. All I could hear was the occasional *beep.....beep.....beep....*of the four Vallons. I tried paying all my attention to the ground at my feet, but I could not help but make quick glances at the far bank towards which we were heading. It was about six or seven hundred meters away. I kept expecting Lee or Gibbs ahead of me to go down in a hail of gunfire, but after twenty minutes, still nothing had happened. Steve was the first one to reach the end, and he turned back to the rest of us shaking his head.
"There's a cliff!" he shouted back.
"What was that sapper Cole?" asked Troopie. He still wasn't using our first names.
"The road ends with a cliff" he repeated. "It drops about ten meters. There was no way a Warrior can get down here".
This information was passed back and discussed among the commanders.

"Just finish up there then," shouted Smudge, "then dress back quick as you can".
The search was wasted. No vehicle could use the road because of the abrupt drop off. Troopie was questioning the infantry commander why his men had risked their lives searching a road that had clearly not even been reconnoitered. I would have been angry too, but I wasn't. I was just happy that it had been another quiet morning.
Later that day we moved onto Middle Hill. My journal records that it took around another hour to walk there along the road, and begin the slow climb up the steep slope. Just before we made the ascent, for some unknown reason to me, we stopped for while in the village at the foot of the hill. Locals had all come out as usual to watch the line of troops, and children lined the roads repeating a few phrases that previous troops had taught them.
"Chocolate! Chocolate!" they would say, pointing to our trouser pockets. Little Steve had given out all his sweets and chocolate to the children who surrounded him, laughing at them and slapping his empty pockets.
"Pen! Pen!" they would then say. Afghan children seemed to be obsessed with pens. "It's for school," Smudge explained, and gave one of the children a pen he had on him. "They need something to write with in class."
"Shampoooooo!" one little boy blurted out.
"What was that?" asked Big Steve, grinning. "What's he asking for?"
"Shampoooooo!" said the little boy again, looking up at us, holding out his hand.
"I think someone's been having fun with this kid" I said. "Shame. NO CHOCOLATE" I said slowly, holding out my hands.
Little Boy looked up at me with huge round eyes. He must have been about six.
"Bam cheri-day?" I asked. Where are the bombs?
He shook his head with his hands held out. He didn't know.
"Taliban cheri-day?" I asked again.
This time he swept his arm in a general direction of the village on the other side of Middle Hill which we wanted to go into. From my map pocket I gave him a ball point pen, and he immediately ran off with it, chased by other children. What a life, I thought. Hidden bombs everywhere, gunfire, Taliban, then us. And all he wants is a

pen so he can learn something in school. It made me think about the school my girlfriend taught in back in the UK.
Middle Hill is really a ridge line that looks over everything. From it, you could see the friendly village we held, the village the Taliban held on the other side, Lockheed Bridge and M4 wadi which we had both uselessly searched, as well as the patrol base which we marched out from each frozen morning. The Taliban had tried building a rudimentary sanger from the boulders strewn over the top of the hill, but had quickly realized that they could not keep it manned because of the threat from the air. But in order to keep us off the hill as well, we assumed they had mined the top with IEDs. The infantry wished to use the hill for their Fire Support Group, but before they could establish more permanent positions with big guns on it, they needed us to make sure it was not booby trapped.
By the time we got to the top of the hill, my shoulders were once again burning from the weight of the ECM. Each time I moved my neck, spasms of pain shot down my spine and my calf muscles ached from the climb. All of us were breathing heavily, taking a look along the top of the ridge which we had to search. The barma team had led the way to the top of the hill, searching a random route in which we followed. Two Warriors were still at the bottom, slowly making their way up the steep slope. The wind-swept ridge looked like no one had been up there for a hundred years, except for the low crumbled wall of stones half way along the top.
As we began searching, it was quickly clear that there was hardly any metal on the top of the hill. All four Vallons, which usually chirped at every piece of buried metal, were silent except for the *beep.....beep......beep....*
I began to think there were no IEDs up here at all, and relaxed slightly. We found none yesterday at the bridge, and none this morning. Maybe I was getting too paranoid? In the way we were configured for this search, I was at the front in the lead but I was fine with that because of the unusual warm happy feeling that I was enjoying. There was no metal for once. The ground in front of me gave absolutely no sign that anyone had been there, and was littered with small rocks on hard ground. Behind us was a Warrior which had its gun trained on the enemy village down the slope. It was a few hundred metres away.
"I-comm says 'They're getting closer'," shouted the signaler.

We all stop.
"You hear that, lads?" shouted Smudge.
"Yeah, thanks," one of us eventually says back. My mind is spinning. There's IEDs up here. I'm the lead man. Closer? What are we getting closer to? What am *I* getting closer to? Where the *fuck* are they? I took a step forward slower, much slower. The ground ahead of me which before seemed so empty and abandoned still seemed empty and abandoned. My confidence is gone. I thought about the little boy down in the village, with his pen. If only my worries were his.
Off to the left, down the hill was the village which the Taliban were in. They were watching us move slowly along the ridge, but were holding their fire until one of us was blown up by one of the bombs they had buried. Then they would open fire with everything they had on the survivors who tried frantically to get tourniquets onto amputated limbs, while pinned down and screaming at the top of their lungs for help.
We worked our way along the ridge in silence, each man concentrating on the strip of ground ahead of him which he has to walk on. Behind us follows Smudge, Big Steve and Troopie, and behind them was the Warrior which occasionally would trundle along a few feet before stopping again. The second Warrior had taken up a position at the start of hill where we had stood an hour ago catching our breath. Some infantry machine gunners had lined the ridge behind us, and more had occupied a smaller hill further up. Everyone had their guns covering the village.
"Find!" cried Lee.
He had just gone down to confirm the only metal tone any of us had hit since we started the search. He quickly uncovered a pressure plate. The relief.
"Well done Lee," says Troopie, slapping him on the back as we all retreat back to the Warrior. The IEDD team are getting their kit ready for the ATO, who is questioning Lee on any details he saw before he starts walking forward with his number two man.
For the next twenty minutes, we all relax and lie in the sun as the ATO sets up his charge to blow up the device. For once, we're not cold. No one is really talking, and Smudge has gone to sleep again.
"It's another cooking pot," says Doug as he comes back. "It's about ten kilos of HME". That was home-made explosives. The Taliban in

Musa Qualeh, it seemed, were still using obsolete high metal IEDs which were easy prey for Vallons. In most other areas, they had long since stopped using metal in their bombs, but instead knew a variety of other material which could not be detected. Around the Minden area, we were lucky.
"Right, everyone get into cover," said the ATO.
"There will be a controlled explosion in one minute" radioed the signaler to all the other troops in the area.
We all lay behind the Warrior, lying flat on the ground. As usual, cameras had been carefully perched between rocks in the direction which the owners had thought was where the IED was buried. Those who could peered carefully between the Warrior's caterpillar tracks to see the explosion.
"Firing! FIRING NOW!"
I felt the shock waves pass through the ground I lay on as the bomb blew up with a loud clap, and a second later, bits of small stones were falling around us, followed by larger chunks of rock. The dust cloud which had billowed out into the sky sank back to earth and engulfed our group who were picking themselves up off the ground. The initial curiosity and excitement of seeing real explosions in a war had by now long been replaced by a mixture of dread and relief. It had become hard not to imagine the immediate consequences of missing an IED and stepping on it and having it detonate. I don't think I was the only man who had begun to think like this. Straight after the initial blast, people would give their opinion on the type of wounds it would have caused. "That would have been both legs," someone would say, or "that's a fatality."

Lee found two more IED's soon afterward his first one. They were both by the crumbling stone wall that the Taliban had erected for a gun position. He had been detailed to clear around the sanger while the three of us carried on past it, unaware that it was where the Taliban had chosen to bury their booby traps.
Because the second and third IED's had been found in quick succession, and because we wanted to get a move on along the ridge, the ATO decided to blow them both up together. I had lost interest in seeing the two holes which had now been unearthed to reveal the entire device. All I cared about at that moment was that for the ten or twenty minutes, I wouldn't have to walk into the unsearched ground

to try and find any others. Smudge and I were both lying on our backs in the sun, listening to the Warrior's engine.

Suddenly everything happened fast. Everyone else in the team had gone over to the holes to take a look at the pressure plates when everywhere, the air exploded. Smudge flipped onto his stomach and had his rifle unclipped in one motion. Without realising it, I had crawled back behind the Warrior to where Smudge was and we both huddled against its tracks. Loud whistles were whining above us, mixed with a long continuous burst of machinegun fire coming from down the slope. Noises like a zip being pulled very quickly were shooting past us and above us. In those first two seconds, I didn't know what was going on, or what to do. I looked up and saw those who had walked out a few moments ago were now sprinting as fast as they could, bent double. My heart was racing, and I seemed incapable of moving.

No one had noticed in those first few moments but all along the ridge behind us from where we had started that day, machine guns were shooting back down into the village. The heavy machine guns were systematically destroying a small building where for a second, I caught a glimpse of what I thought was someone firing up at us. The Taliban, who had initially relied on their IEDs to kill us, had instead spent the day watching us find one booby trap after the other. They could see where we were and were either too frustrated, or were hoping that one of us would panic and take cover among the rocks, where there might have been more bombs. Suddenly there was another *bang!* different from the other noises.

"What the hell's that?!" I shouted at Smudge.

"What?" He couldn't hear me.

"What is that?"

"The canons," he yelled, pointing up at the gun turrets. Between the tracks of the Warrior, I could follow the tracer round flying down the slope to slam into a wall. It collapsed in a sudden small puff of brown dust.

Troopie was doing his best to explain to everyone amidst all the firing what exactly he thought was going on, but it looked like no one was taking any notice.

Our ATO, who had been cut off from us in the opening bursts of the contact, had initially dived to the ground. Now that our guns had silenced the enemy's fire, he decided now was a good time to detonate the two IED's he had prepared to blow. He emerged from the earth where he had squashed himself into and dived into the crater from Lee's first IED. He was signalling that he was about to detonate. He was very close. We could make out his cries over the crackling and snapping and whistling. *"Firing....ring....ow!*

Just behind him it seemed, the two bombs blew up together. The ground in all directions simultaneously shot up a layer of dust as the shock wave passed through the earth, and rocks the size of cricket balls were flung up into the air, only to come raining down again for the next few seconds.

Doug stayed in his hole until all firing up the slope stopped as the Warriors continued destroying whatever they aimed at. Then suddenly the shooting stopped. In the wake of such massive volume of noise a second ago, it was eerily silent. Down the slope, a building had collapsed, and trees were smouldering.

"I think we'll have a bit of a soak period after that," said Troopie, grinning and everyone burst into laughter. Sometimes it was best to sit and wait and see what happens before venturing out again. But nothing else happened that day. We watched the village through our Susats for a while afterwards, but there were no movements, and their radios were silent. It was a good sign. We searched another fifty meters or so that day before the light began to fail and we decided to call it a day.

It was another two hours before we arrived back at the patrol base, having walked the distance from Middle Hill along the secured road we'd passed that morning. Everyone was hobbling like cripples. By the time we passed the front gate, all I could think about was taking off the weight I was carrying on my shoulders. My neck burned with every move of my head, and I could feel stabs of pain in both shoulders for a few minutes after I had finally removed the ECM and body armour. The soles of both my feet had 'hot spots,' which felt just like blisters, making it painful to walk. Smudge looked done in as well, and had exhaustion etched on his face. Everyone was weary and ready for bed. We hadn't been able to wash since we arrived at Minden. There wasn't much of a washing system yet, and soldiers were bathing out of buckets of icy water every few days.

We spent dinner that night inside a caved-in room of the compound,

standing over a small fire in which dinner was being cooked. On the fire was an ammunition tin filled with water which was slowly being heated up. Bags of rations had been carefully inserted into the water to fit the maximum number in at once. Everyone was staring at the flames slowly heating the water, watching our rations boiling and warming our hands over the fire. Since the sun had gone down, the temperature had dropped rapidly. There wasn't a cloud in the night sky, which was lit up by a canopy of bright stars. It was going to be another cold night. Soldiers with head torches strapped to their heads were walking around in the darkness, hands deep in the pockets of their softie jackets and heads smothered by woollen beanies. Gibbs and Little Steve, always together, stood in the corner of the room, talking about the events of the day and speculating if we would be going back up the hill the next day.
"You think we'll be going up that hill tomorrow?" I asked.
"Don't see why to be honest with you," said Big Steve. "They can smash that village from where we searched today."
"I reckon they'll have us back up there" Gibbs said. "They're basically going to use and abuse us for as long as we're here."
"Wonder where we'll be for Christmas," someone remarked.
"The chopper could come get us tomorrow," I said. "We always get told last."
It had been playing on all our minds. No one wanted to get left in some cold, bleak patrol base with no fresh food, no hot water, and most importantly, no Facebook. We had no idea how long we would be left at Minden for, even though each night Troopie had been trying to get in touch with the commanders at Bastion to find out what would happen with us. As far as we were concerned, both the bridge and the wadi were a waste of time. We'd risked our lives, for nothing.
At that moment, Troopie got back from the O Group he had been attending with the other commanders. We could tell from the way he walked in that there was more to be done. He had a map in his hands and went straight for a flat surface in long enthusiastic strides.
"Gather round lads," he tells us. We huddle round, inwardly groaning. No one is going back. There's more to be done. On the map at our feet, we can see all the features we had been walking over the last couple of days. Troopie was talking about Middle Hill again.

"They want us to go up there and extend the track for the Warriors, so they can have a bit of space," he explains. "They want a turning circle...here", he says pointing with a bit of grass to the end of the ridge, "and they need the track way widened. So, pretty much same as today."
The mood is ominous.
"Why do they need it widened?" asked Smudge immediately. "For what? All they need to do is drive up and down a single lane, like what that Warrior was doing today."
"Why do they need a turning circle?" someone else asked. "Can't they just reverse, or pivot on their tracks?"
"It's what they said they wanted. I had a go at them for the other tasks they gave us to do. The hill is the main effort now. They want to make it into a more permanent position so they can dominate the area around that other village we saw today...."
But I was no longer listening. My hopes had been crushed. The Sea King coming to rescue us had seemed a small hope, but it was what I had counted on when Troopie had been away at the O Group. I didn't want to go out on the ground again tomorrow. I wanted to lie in and sleep and wake up smelling clean in a warm bed with aromatic freshly ground coffee. I still had not gotten used to the coffee sachets that come in the ration boxes. I could only drink them when it was really hot, and with lots of powdered milk.
Later that night, I finally got to take my boots off, pour foot powder onto some precious fresh socks and get into my doss bag.
Within a minute, I was shivering.

Our sniper spotted Taliban on Middle Hill the next morning. We had been patrolling out from the base again, and slowly making our way up to the village at the foot of the hill when the man two places in front of me suddenly stopped and raised his rifle up to the ridge of the hill, just in time to see a figure disappear beyond the skyline. This information was passed along the patrol, and made us angry when we heard it.
"Aren't those bastards keeping an eye on that hill?" someone shouted, referring to the outpost that sat on an adjacent hill just behind it. It consisted of nothing more than a small ring of hesco wall, surrounded with a small perimeter fence of razor sharp danet-

coil. There were a few gun positions, but that was it. The unfortunate soldiers manning that post slept under ponchos behind their wall, or under the stars. If it was cold for us sleeping in a tent back at the patrol base, life must have been freezing for them.
The discovery of Taliban on the hill so early in the morning put us all on edge. No doubt they had been checking to see how many of their bombs we had found the previous day, and looking for signs of blood on the ground to see if they had hit anyone. The obvious possibility no one wanted to think about was that they were burying more devices before we go there.

Up on Middle Hill. Same place as yesterday. The ridge had once again gone back to seeming empty and abandoned, like no one had set foot there since Alexander the Great's hoplites marched through this country thousands of years ago. How many armies had invaded Afghanistan anyway? I wondered as we continued yesterday's work. Once again, the ground, void of any kind of metal, stayed silent. We were nearing the far end of the ridge, and despite yesterday's contact, I was feeling okay with searching for once. It was promising to be a quick and easy day. The infantry could have their damn extended super highway complete with turning circles, lay-bys and service stops. The Taliban had so far left us alone, or maybe they were all still dead? Except the man we saw up here at dawn. He definitely wasn't dead. Just what exactly was he doing up here anyway?
"I-comm says, 'they're coming to the others'," shouted the signaller. The Taliban are watching our progression again.
"There's more up here?" I hear Little Steve ask no one in particular. He and I are at the front, moving hesitantly forward, reluctant to distance ourselves from the protective Warrior behind. I wondered what we must look like through the sights of the PKM that someone down in the village was studying us through. It was like a scene in Jaws where the camera films the unsuspecting swimmer on the surface from below, showing what the shark sees as it moves in during the last few seconds of the victim's life.
A machinegun began firing. To the left. From the village. I had dived to the ground without even thinking about it, and was hugging the earth as flat as I could. My Vallon had somehow ended up behind me and was making the continuous *beeeeeeeeeeeep* that happens when you drop it. I looked up ahead of me and saw Little

Steve lying face down on the ground. Was he dead? No, his boots were moving as he pivoted around on his stomach to face me. He was about ten metres away.
"Steve!" I screamed. He didn't hear me. He was trying to disentangle himself from his rifle strap while keeping as low as possible.
"Steve!"
"Yeah!" There was another burst of gunfire, though this time it wasn't at us anymore.
"You alright mate?" I shouted. Stones were digging into my elbows and knees. I wanted to merge myself into the ground.
"Is Steve okay?" Smudge called out from the Warrior. They had all taken cover behind the armour.
"Yeah," Little Steve called back. "You?"
"Yeah." I turned back. "He's okay," I shouted, before turning back to face him. We were both still lying flat on the ground and trying to keep ourselves from straying into any unsearched areas. "We got to get back to the Warrior."
"I know" he said.
"You go first."
"Fuck off," he said. "You go first."
Gibbs and Lee had been a distance behind us when the firing began and had been able to crawl back to the cover of the Warrior, where the rest of our group were. The Warrior was firing back with its main cannon. The firing coming up the slope from the village seemed to have died as soon as the Warrior's guns began shooting. I felt a pang of unease before deciding to chance it and began sprinting back, bent double. It's surprising how fast you can move with your body bent forwards at ninety degrees while carrying all your kit. That's what I was thinking as I ran for cover, skidding in behind the tracks of the armoured vehicle like a baseball player diving for a home run, and bruising my thighs over the stony ground. Then Steve took his chances and came sprinting in, also bent over double. Smudge, the only one of us who had been shot at before we arrived in Afghanistan, was giving out some helpful advice to Steve as he dashed towards him.
"Lower.....lower.....lower," he was saying, shaking his head in disapproval at Steve as he shot past him behind the Warrior. "You need to get lower when you run," he said in exasperation.
Now we were back with the others behind the armour, we could

relax a little. Some Afghan soldiers had occupied a hamlet the previous night on the other side of the Taliban-held village. It was they who had been pinning the Taliban down and drawing their fire, allowing everyone up on Middle Hill to run back into cover. The Taliban were now surrounded on three sides, but they weren't going anywhere.

Nothing had happened now for ten minutes. One of the infantry had been shot in the leg in the initial exchange of gunfire, but he had been evacuated very quickly off the hill, watched enviously by everyone else who had to stay and wait for the Taliban's next move. I remember feeling a flash of extreme jealousy. He'll be home in the UK before Christmas, I thought. I had an uneasy feeling that it was too late for me to get shot in the leg.

The Warrior's guns had stopped shooting, and we lay strung out in the sun behind it in the searched ground, watching the village through the scopes of our rifles. I didn't know what was happening, or why no one was shooting or moving. Maybe the commanders were all discussing on the radios what the next move was going to be? Maybe we were waiting for an Apache to give us some air cover?

Helicopters were in such short supply in Afghanistan that whenever commanders on the ground did manage to get some air cover, they only had a few minutes with which to use them before they would get sent off to another part to help another unit in a tight spot.

Through my Susat, nothing was moving down in the village. Were there civilians? Was that why we weren't shooting anymore? There were several windows in the mud-coloured buildings, no bigger than black pencil dots, and quite suddenly from out of one of the pencil dots came a glint of reflected sunlight.

"Someone's watching us," Gibbs said next to me. He'd also seen it. Why weren't they shooting at us? I could only guess that they were enjoying the past few minutes of peace as much as I was.

The two sides continued watching each other on that forgotten hill and un-named village for the following hour we stayed on that hill. I never did know why the fighting stopped before it really did begin, why everyone involved suddenly seemed content to just watch each other through telescopic lenses. Maybe they were waiting for us to make a mistake and walk onto a bomb we didn't know about. Maybe they were praying. Maybe we had spotted civilians down there. No

one told us, and none of us cared anymore because we'd been just been told by Troopie that we were going to get picked up by the Sea King that afternoon. That bit of information made all interest in the impending fire-fight disappear instantly. It was all that mattered.
We'd searched the safe lane that infantry had asked for, and now they knew that other devices were still lurking somewhere up on that hill, they knew to make sure the perimeter was always well marked.
In another hour we had descended that hill and were on our way back to the patrol base.
Behind us, in the village where the children begged us for chocolate and shampoo, I could see those same kids flying their kites.
If only our worries were theirs.

We're back at the main camp at Musa Qualeh.
One of the first things everyone did when we arrived back at our tent was to grab a towel and some fresh warm clothes to change into straight away and head towards the shower-tent. No one had washed while we were at Minden, which was only a three-minute helicopter flight away. I stood under the scorching hot water for as long as I dared before letting in the next guy waiting in turn behind me.
Later on that evening, I'm sitting in one of the toilets, having finally managed to place the wagbag dead square in the toilet seat hole in the light of a head torch. Firing breaks out from the perimeter. It starts in small uncertain waves of noise, like thunder before a storm, and echoes through the night air before stopping, throwing the fading reverberations through the valley. Then it erupts again, louder, faster. At least two machine guns are firing in short and sometimes even longer bursts, which suggested that someone was either panicking or overexcited. The two soldiers in the cubicles either side of me have also stopped what they're doing as we all listen, trying to work out what's going on. It's not unusual to hear background shooting. There's always someone shooting at someone else, somewhere within earshot. But the volume of noise had grown considerably in the last minute, in which everyone sitting in the toilets had to decide if they should finish up before people outside began yelling "Stand To! Stand To!"
During our stay in Minden, one of the nearby American patrol bases had very nearly been overrun by a Taliban assault one night. Was this the start of an attack? Leaning against the cubicle door is my

rifle and in the trouser pocket around my ankles is a magazine. But just as suddenly as it started, the shooting stopped. It was as if someone had turned off the taps. There was complete silence.

23/12/09 MSQ DC
Back at MSQ. Some new Brigadier has new rules. Neat uniform to be worn. Haircuts and no sideburns. No black boots – they must be brown. Everyone laughs in disbelief. Then starts bitching. Airheads. Never been out on the ground. They do know there's a real war on? I thank God I've got my legs.

An explosion rocks my world. Where am I? What's happened? Smudge had lost both his arms at the elbows, and he's lying on his back, screaming.
I wake up.

Christmas Day.
Opened all the care packages and basically spent the day chilling out and stuffing our faces. Gave one of the boxes to Tom C, who came here yesterday. Spent the day mostly watching movies with him.
We had a nice Christmas lunch, which was real nice. Spoke to family and Anna on phone. Also went to church service this evening.
The power is out. Tent is freezing cold. Everyone is wearing head torches.

Boxing Day should be okay. Nothing on tomorrow. But we have another op the next day - a resupply. Hoping we'll just be going as QRF. Yesterday we were called out by some guys opening route Green. Someone had a single hit on a vallon without even confirming it. As we approached, all ready to go, it became apparent what the story was. Everyone swears and curses. Haven't even confirmed? ATO went to the marked off area (was in the middle of nowhere) and digs up a nail.
Cheers for spoiling Christmas Eve.

That Christmas spent at Musa Qualeh District Command was a day everyone was able to relax, because Patrol Minimise had been called. That meant that no one would be going out on the ground unless absolutely necessary. The commanders just didn't want

anyone becoming a casualty on Christmas Day, and bringing a family emergency to some unsuspecting family back home in the UK.
Soldiers broke open their Santa suits that seemed to appear from nowhere. Everyone was walking around with shoe boxes of Christmas items that had been sent to the troops by the public. In one tent, Santa came and put up his *Santa's Grotto* sign and soldiers started queuing up to sit on his lap while another took a digital photo which would be emailed to families back home. In the shoe box they gave me were an assortment of chocolates, biscuits, shower gel, tooth paste, cheese, and, most important of all, tinned haddock fillets in tomato sauce. There was also a letter from a little boy whose school had contributed to packing the Christmas presents. Each line of writing was in a different colour of felt tip maker, and below was a drawing of a tall smiling soldier holding hands with small smiling children on either side of him.

Christmas lunch was done by the chefs working all morning in the field kitchens at the back of the cookhouse tent. They had worked hard to produce a Christmas meal for everyone. The army had made great efforts to make sure all the soldiers had a good meal. Mashed potatoes, roast chicken and beef, sausages wrapped in bacon. Each platoon took turns in the cook house throughout the day, slinging rifles behind chairs or placed carefully under the table, and wearing the delicate paper hats that come in Christmas crackers.
I spent the rest of the day with another one of friends from training I had bumped into, whose name was Tom. He had been sent to the Musa Qualeh as a fitter, and was in charge of maintaining all the heavy-duty engines. I gave him one of my care-packages, seeing that I had two and he didn't have any, and we spent the afternoon watching *The Muppets Christmas* on his DVD player, and exchanging war-stories.

We settled into winter life at Musa Qualeh. It rained most days, filling the water-logged ground with enormous puddles that never went away. The nights were always pitch black when the clouds blocked the light from the moon and stars, and often meant you could not see the tent pegs or cords which anchored the ten men tents against the wind. Rifles became rusty very quickly and constantly had to be checked and cleaned. Inside our tents we tried

hanging the damp laundry on washing lines which we strung across the room, but nothing every dried properly and our clothes took on a new damp, mouldy smell. The tents themselves were freezing, especially at night when the temperature dropped dramatically. We had managed to get our hands on some sort of heater, but it was too small and the tent too big for it to ever be effective.
During the day, if we were not called out on the ground, we sat around without much to do. There was one main concrete building at Musa Qualeh DC, three storeys high, and that's where the ops room was, along with all the other war rooms where the officers discussed their orders. The telephones and internet connections were there too. Whenever we could, we booked a time slot on the phones or an old laptop which would surely fall apart at any moment. Soldiers were always sitting there, checking their Facebook pages, while one or two others would be leaning against the wall outside patiently waiting their turn.
A row of phone booths stood to one side, with the entrance to each wooden cubicle covered by a curtain. Inside was a stool, and telephone sitting on a wooden shelf. The wooden walls of each booth were covered with graffiti, usually of soldiers expressing their opinions of the Cavalry unit who were in charge of Musa Qualeh. The House Hold Cavalry, it seemed, were unpopular, even with their own men. One soldier had summed up what everyone thought about the regulation haircuts and side burns length which the Cavalry were trying to enforce.

"We don't give a fuck about sideburns. We got more important things to worry about like keeping our balls and our legs."

A few of their officers had apparently inquired about the search team's dress. A few of us had bought our own brown fleeces as a supplementary layer of winter clothing, and because it was non-regulation, it came up in an O Group one evening. Troopie told them in no uncertain terms that his lads had far more to worry about doing high risk search than worrying about dress. They left us alone after that.
Whenever we had no jobs to do, everyone would gradually relax for the day and hope we were not going to get called out on the ground. When we weren't out on the ground, we were always on QRF.

Everyone would either read, or go to the outside gym, or watch a film on one of the laptops, knowing that with each passing hour, the less our chances became of getting a call out. If we got to about three in the afternoon, then we knew we were home safe. It would be too late. By the time we actually arrived at a location and began searching, the light would be failing. If we got to that time in the afternoon, then we really could relax.

The next concern everyone would have would be about the next day. Were we out on the ground? In would come Troopie after his O Group, his entrance immediately grabbing everyone's attention, looking to him with the un-asked question.

"We're on QRF tomorrow."

Relief. No danger tomorrow. That was all we needed to hear. I'd go back to my game of Risk I was playing with Gibbs, watching him try to formulate a strategy. He still hadn't worked out that Australia was the key to winning the game. Although I'm not showing it, I'm deeply relieved, and very grateful.

Other times, it would be different. In would come Troopie after his O Group, his entrance immediately grabbing everyone's attention, looking to him the un-asked question.

"We have a task tomorrow…."

But I'm not really listening to the next few details. I've immediately lost interest in Risk. I don't care about Australia. I don't feel like playing anymore.

Most of the tasks we did in that area were dealing with bombs that had already been found. We would perform our search procedures, making it safe for the ATO to do his work, usually blowing up the device. Then we would search carefully for any more secondary devices along the stretch of road. One IED found along a main road had held up local traffic for hours as we searched a path for the ATO in the rain. The locals patiently waited in their cars for us to return their community to normal. Occasionally a man would leave the road and walk out a bit into the field and squat, covering himself with his robes as he relieved himself. After the explosion, and after we had checked there were no more IEDs waiting to blow them and their families up, we would wave them through. Normal cars now seemed so flimsy to us, who were by now used to driving around in enormous armoured V-shaped hulls. I didn't like to think of the children sitting on the seats with nothing to stop the force of the blast

from travelling upwards, into them.
We once passed the scene of a car that had struck an IED, or an old Soviet mine – because the road ran past a legacy minefield from the Soviet era. The vehicle had been blown to pieces and was strewn out along the road in all directions. A grave was next to it, a linear mound of earth with three poles erected at one end, sticking out like crows feet, with multi coloured ribbons flying from them.

We've spent most of today guarding the main road for CLP – a Combat Logistic Patrol. We're in the huge dried-up wadi, sat around our Mastiff. Everyone has their turn at stag in the gunner's turret behind the heavy machine gun, but apart from that there was nothing to do all day. Whenever traffic comes our way, we halt them before they get too close and they automatically dismount their motor bikes, lift up their clothes to show their bare stomach, and turn around. The Afghans don't even wait for our instructions. Earlier that day the long convoy had passed us by. It was mixed with both armoured vehicles and four by fours driven by the ANA, with ANA soldiers in the back and flying Afghan flags. One of our trucks had been blown up just behind the rise where we couldn't see. But it was nothing serious. The three men in the front had had back injuries and one had broken his leg, but that was it.
The rest of the day was pretty boring, with us all waiting to be told we could collapse back to the FOB.
Finally Smudge announced he needed to go. There was absolutely nowhere he could have gone for privacy, and even if there was, he wasn't about to wonder off. There had been no traffic for about ten minutes, so off he went around the corner of the Mastiff with a wagbag. Full body armour, helmet and rifle, with his pants around his ankles as he squats down and tries to hold the wagbag in position before he relieves himself.
At that moment, a motorbike with an entire family pulls up to our stag point. They see Smudge and stop, turn off the engine and start watching him. The boy sitting in front of his dad on the saddle begins laughing. The wife behind the father begins laughing. Then the father starts laughing, and so do we. Smudge, trapped in his unescapable situation also begins laughing. After about a minute, the Chohgee family starts their engine, wave goodbye and drive away.
I didn't think anything of it at the time, but looking back on that day,

the craziest thing was that no one seemed too interested in the IED strike that took out the truck earlier.

We are on another op. We've been travelling for a few hours and finally made it to a satellite station by night fall. The small outpost was on the outskirts of a sizable town in the area called Woquat. The enormous Mastiffs slowly crept into the confines of the walls like cattle coming into their kraal, guided by a man in front of each vehicle holding a glowing cylume for the driver to see. We each clambered out from the mouth of the open doors at the back, eyes adjusting to the dark and trying to see what kind of place we would be spending the night. It was hard to see anything. A large force of Taliban was still in Woquat, and strictly no lights or fires were allowed. Everyone was working in the eerie-green light of cylumes attached to their helmets. We unloaded all our kit from the Mastiff and piled it against the wall, trying to keep out of the way. Everyone immediately looked for a comfortable spot where they could unpack their roll mat and sleeping bag, and claim that bit of ground for the night before it got taken. Lee and I found a suitable patch of ground, and after clearing away all the larger rocks, erected the poncho overhead in case it would rain.

We emerged from beneath our shelter to find the other shadows huddled in a group, discussing in low voices the next most important thing on our minds.

"Where's the cookhouse?" one shadow asked.

"It's in there," murmured one of the infantry shadows as it walked past, pointing to the single small building in the compound.

Everyone instinctively made their way to the black hole that was the door, and disappeared inside, as if sucked in by a giant fish.

Inside was a cave.

It was seductively warm, and dark, and wafting with smells or unwashed bodies, cooked dinner and smoke. The room opened out into a dark cavern illuminated by three small candles which sent light flickering uneasily into the farthest corners. Undisturbed lines of white candle wax were streaked across the long table, and spilled over the edge to form thin stalagmites reaching the earthen floor. Against the side of one wall was a small fire heating an ammo tin filled with water. It was already full of rations belonging to the soldiers who were there, sitting around the table. In the half light,

people are there waiting for their food to get hot, or for enough space in the ammo tin to squeeze their packet in.
In my memory everything in that place was darkness and shadows. The infantry we were with were trying to dominate the town which must have not been too far away, and had suspicions of IEDs being buried in some key places they wanted to occupy. They first wanted them checked.
That night as we lay sleeping on the rocky ground staring up at the stars, the fear and the loneliness.

The next day the infantry moved into the town. We had clambered well before sunrise into the Mastiffs and drove the short distance to where we de-bused. So far there had been no contact with the enemy, so we got to work on the first area. Because we didn't know where the enemy were in those moments before fighting begins, we stayed alert and kept paired up, with one man searching and another following a few metres behind to protect him. None of us knew what the grander picture was on what the chain of command wanted with the town, how much we occupied or why it was important. All that mattered was to keep our team safe.
Little Steve found an IED. It was in an archway frequented by Afghan soldiers. It turned out to be a "come on", a lure of a high metal content of some kind like an emptied-out mortar bomb. The hope was that an inexperienced ATO would focus on it, thinking he was safe, when the real killer was still undetected, in his immediate vicinity. Fortunately, our ATO knew what he was dealing with and soon found the real device a few inches away. He decided to blow it up in situ, and the resulting explosion collapsed the archway, which must have been there a hundred years.
Within a few seconds, a warning came over the net of impending contact. Women and children were seen leaving the town. A minute later, a burst of firing broke out. Like all other contacts we had been in, no one knew where it was coming from, but it wasn't at us. The town remained exactly the same, a deaf person wouldn't have known the difference. To our front, where the infantry had gone in, there was a maze of compounds and alleyways. The sound of gunfire permeated the scene. Our second area to seemed to be on the other end of town. A few of the infantry led us through a series of alleys and open ground, and about fifteen of us made our way past all the

fighting which seemed to be first to our front, then to our left, then to our rear. There were several heavy detonations and at times a continual crackling of automatic weapons, then a lull where the town returned to silence. By the time we got to our objective, air support had been called in. An A-10 could be seen flying circles overhead in the brilliant blue morning sky. Occasionally it dived for a strafing run, firing its Gatling machine gun. It sounded like an enormous fart coming from the sky.
We lay in the ICP, looking up at the blue sky and seeing the smoke trails from the strafing runs and hearing the infantry snap shooting a hundred metres away. Doug had blown up the two IEDs that the infantry wanted removed, which added to the noise that morning. Later, in the safety of the FOB, we ate our lunch between two Mastiffs. The fight was still going on and there were snipers and heavy machine guns on the Hesco towers shooting into the town. I stood in the Mastiff's turret, looking at the town through binoculars, watching the dust and smoke drift lazily into the sky. We all knew full well that civilians still lived here. I wondered how people in the UK would react if a pitched battle was being fought in their town.

New Year's Eve, 2009. The Chinook drops us back to Bastion. The Daff picks us up at the flightline and the driver wishes us happy new year. We had no idea what day it was. Not long after we had dumped our kit in our tents, everyone present in the CIED lines are called into the welfare tent. When we had all gathered, they announced another casualty. He had been a pretty good soldier, and had passed P Company and the Commando course. He had been casevaced to Bastion, but had died later than night, on New Year's Eve.

6
BABAJI

91 days remaining.

Its three o'clock in the morning. So cold. There's a bad metallic taste in my mouth, and my stomach is empty. All I want to do is hide. Go down deeper into the warm, toasty doss bag and just lie still. Maybe no one will see me. In the dark, shapes are moving around. Doss bags are being packed away, people are putting on their boots and getting their kit in order. Here and there, murmurs. If you're clever, you'd go to bed with your kit already in order right besides where you sleep so you know where everything is in the dark.

On this morning, we're going out on an op. The area south of us was Taliban-controlled neighbourhood, and this op was all about show of force. Someone much higher up the chain of command had thought it would be a good idea if the locals could see we could go anywhere we liked, anytime we liked. That way, we'd be seen to be stronger than the Taliban, and they'd start to trust us to protect them when they told us where those damn IEDs were.

On that morning, well before daybreak, the three main patrols – multiples - were all strung out by the entrance to the patrol base in their marching orders. They'd all leave separately, taking different routes to the target compound, zig-zagging all over the map in order to be as unpredictable as possible, and finally converge on a location just before dawn.

We'd have about two hours to get there.

It's cold, dark, and we're carrying a lot of weight. As we leave, we cock our rifles and tuck it into the crook of the arm, shrug the ECM into a comfier position on my back and begin following the man a few metres ahead.

Just before we set off on that op, Gibbs mentioned the news to me. Doug was dead. They'd all been told the previous night after the O Group, but I was off somewhere, and somehow, I didn't get that bit. We had left Musa Qualeh two weeks ago but Doug and his team stayed on while a new team arrived while we were moved on to Babaji. He'd been killed trying to defuse an IED, and stepped on a secondary one. He had died shortly after in the Mastiff.

Usually on foot patrols you'd have many stops. Sometimes it's because the commander is trying to work out our position on the map, sometimes it's the lead searcher at the head of the file who is working out the best route to take. Sometimes it's an irrigation ditch that everyone up ahead is trying to negotiate, if possible, without getting wet. Each time the patrol stops, every man takes a knee, facing left, right, left, right. And there you kneel, feeling the weight you're carrying bear down onto your knee and into the ground, trying to make out features in front of you. There's a bitterly cold wind sweeping through the line of soldiers. You still can't see much in the dark, but the Taliban don't like getting up this early in the morning. Eventually, after kneeling, waiting, seeing the man in front of you turn and pat you on the shoulder, getting up, walking a few steps, stopping and kneeling again, you can finally see the irrigation ditch that's been holding everyone up.

It's too big to jump over, so everyone is getting wet. The water is ice cold, and you can feel it flood your boots and submerge your toes as you wade through it. Some ditches were narrow enough to jump across, even though you're carrying all that weight. You take a leap and as soon as you landed on the other side, you'd have to grab frantically in the dark for some reeds or branches, or anything to pull you forward so you don't fall back. Always make sure you stay in the searched ground. One foot might go in the water and get wet, and that would just ruin your day because 'once you're piss-wrapped, you're piss-wrapped.'

Before flying out to Afghanistan, we'd been issued water proof boots, which would be ideal on cold patrols like this where there's the risk of getting soaked. But during that operation, we'd been ordered by some visiting high-ranking General that all troops were not allowed to wear them because they were black, while the rest of our battle dress was all brown. It has to match. Everyone had to wear brown desert boots, that let water right in when you can't jump far enough.

By five in the morning, just short of two hours later, we had converged on an abandoned compound that last night's O Group had decided should be our Form Up Point. Soldiers from other patrols who had arrived before us were already there squatting against the compound wall, trying to stay warm. Because of the secrecy, fires were forbidden. There were plenty of ANA soldiers there too, clustered together, and hanging heavily around those groups was a strong smell of weed.

By now I'm not scared anymore. I'm just freezing. Everyone has frozen boots from those irrigation ditches, and I can't feel my toes. My team is all standing huddled together, stamping their feet. I'm wriggling my feet vigorously, taking it in turns to do left and then right. After about half an hour, they seemed a little bit warmer. Initially when we arrived, the first thought was to find a place and get some sleep once we found out we would be there for a while. But lying down had proven too cold, and your body starts to shiver too violently to sleep, so eventually we just resigned ourselves to waiting for the infantry cordon to get into place before we go in and raid the target compound. What I'm really waiting for though is for the sun to come up. It's by now broken the horizon, and shining over the wall that we're huddled behind for cover, and warming up the ground it falls on. As it gets higher, the line of sunshine gets closer to our group...but actually walking out to it and standing in the sun is out of the question. That's not searched ground. No one wants to really risk searching it. It's better to stay frozen.

Much later on that day as it finally got warmer, with the infantry in place to cover us, the Search Team was finally called. The compound that this whole raid was about was owned by a local Taliban leader, but despite everyone getting up early to catch them, they'd already just fled. We could hear them over the radio talking to each other as they watched us move into their home, and the tangeeman would tell everyone what they were saying about us.

"They're going into the house"

"Are you in place yet?"

The ANA had done a quick check on one compound that was safer, because there were kids and livestock roaming around freely. But they wouldn't enter the one next to it. It was empty. "They think there are IEDs in that one, that's why they don't want to go in". And this is where the fear suddenly comes back. I never let on to anyone else how scared I was the whole time I was in Afghan. Entering a doorway. For simple tasks like this that could very likely be your last, an enormous amount of caution and concentration is needed. Always the same questions: am I going to blow up? Will I miss something? Will someone else die because of me?

The team goes about our business the way we'd been trained, making it safe for the others to follow. No finds. The commander wanted the rooms searched. There were three of them. Two of them were storage rooms and were filled to the brim with all sorts of junk. There were mounds of stored sacks of grain, farming tools, pots, pans, thick wads of old papers with writing which could say anything. A hiding place for a cache of weapons could be anywhere, but so could a trip wire, triggering a bomb. It all had to be thoroughly searched, very carefully.

Going through someone else's room - the enemy's room- was a sobering experience. On that task I remember rummaging through this Taliban commander's belongings and came across a photograph album. Inside were pictures of him and his family. He's standing there between his two daughters, an arm on each shoulder, smiling. They're in a garden. None of it seemed real.

In another room, Little Steve found their hide. It was a hidden hole tucked away somewhere, large enough to conceal a rifle, but it was empty. Apart from that, we didn't find anything else. There were loads of documents which we gave to the tangeeman to interpret, but nothing that I can remember that stuck out. Just having to put things back the way we'd found it and trying to remember what went where and trying not to damage anything. It's funny how you can get caught up in such trivial stuff like that. Trying to be respectful in someone's home who you would be expected to kill if you saw him in a contact.

Long after I left Afghan, bought a house, married and settled into a life of my own, we were burgled. Strangers were in our house, rummaging through our things, emptying out our draws. It made me think of raids like these in a different way. Seeing the enemy in a family photograph. What the hell are we doing here? But again, I didn't say anything.

I'm glad we didn't wreck that guy's house.

Much later on that day, the Taliban, who had been restraining themselves so far, finally snapped. The search team had done their job, and quite frankly, we were all waiting to collapse back to the patrol base and take our boots off. In the meantime, we're lying on our backs on a gravel mound in the sun, watching aircraft fly overhead. Smudge is asleep. He's snoring again. The rest of us had just noticed piles of shit everywhere and realised that this must be the village public toilets when suddenly, further on up, firing breaks out. Everyone instinctively flips onto their stomachs, grabbing their rifles, but almost immediately it's clear that it's not at us. You can hear rounds flying overhead, *whiizzzzzzzzz. pshhhheeeeeeeoooowww......*but we're safely tucked out of the way. In any case, the infantry had brought up their Vikings that were moving into position and firing back. It was all a laid-back affair. Engines idling. The occasional shooting - their fire popping and whizzing our way, more engine rumbles, more aircraft noises, more sunshine, more waft of shit.

"Gibbs mate, watch where you putting your boots." And then our heavy machine guns and grenade machine guns opening up in short bursts back at them.

You couldn't really move anywhere, not so much because of the bullets overhead, but more because of the piles of human shit we had discovered. It really didn't feel like a war.

The firing died down after that. One of our Vikings had been hit by an RPG, but because of the bar armour surrounding it, it didn't go off but went cart-wheeling off it. Bar armour is what every vehicle is surrounded by. It looks like a cage around the whole vehicle, and it's to stop RPGs from detonating when they hit the gaps between the bars, in a way catching it.

Later on, that day I remember starting the long walk back to PB3. We got contacted down the road quite suddenly again, and this time it was more at us and a lot more intense. The whole multiple went from a slow walk to a quick dive onto the ground, eventually rolling off the road into the deep irrigation canal. I can remember my boots scrambling up the muddy slope while I'm sliding down, still trying not get them wet because they had finally dried from that morning, and it was starting to get cold again.

Cracks overhead. The shooting was coming from across the field. As usual, I couldn't see them. But our sniper could. We could hear him firing back with his high-powered rifle while orders were shouted down the line for everyone to start peeling up the canal while the rest covered us. A lot of people were shouting. We were wading waist deep in water, but I'm not noticing it being cold. I've gone from freezing back to plain scared again, trying not to trip on submerged

branches while keeping my head down, as well as trying to move as fast as possible with ECM on my back. I was more concerned with tripping up and sprawling face down in that water, and holding up the people behind me.
After that contact, it seemed that the Chohgees were also getting cold, because they suddenly disappeared and left us alone on our long collapse back to the patrol base. Everyone had reached the safety of two compounds where we had taken cover, and busy re-organising ourselves. The commander of our patrol was furious at the how that had all gone.
"Everyone shut the fuck up!" he was yelling, and that brought a subdued atmosphere among the soldiers in his immediate surroundings, like naughty school boys being scolded by a teacher. People were just coming in, getting their breath back, dripping wet. The search team was once again lying in the grass off to one side, riding out the verbal abuse, secretly shaking our heads and rolling our eyes at each other. Just waiting for orders to get going again. What pissed the commander off was the fact that it seemed like just two or maybe even one gunman who had been shooting at us, pinning us down in that cold water, and there were more than twenty of us. The army back then had been issued with a new policy called Courageous Restraint. Soldiers are not allowed to shoot indiscriminately at the undergrowth without identifying their targets. Although there were more of us than them, we couldn't really do much if we couldn't see them. Courageous Restraint meant that we couldn't open up on the opposite field. Instead, it meant taking cover and get shot at.

It took a long time to get back that evening because each multiple stops every now and again and waits for the other one to catch up, taking it in turns to cover each other. When we finally got back, I was running on fumes. The weight of the ECM on my shoulders was burning and no amount of shrugging helped. There's mud clumped around my boots, making them twice the size. Smudge is the man ahead of me and I can tell by the way he's walking that he's feeling the same as me. As the team commander, he's designated himself to carry the heaviest ECM. Thanks to those Chohgees shooting at us earlier, no one can feel their soaking toes again.

We joined the queue at the unloading bay, and unloaded our weapons, checking the chamber. Fire off the action. Pick up the round that I never fired that day and put it back in the magazine that I didn't need as I trudge towards the tent where I finally dumped that damn ECM and take off my body armour. Straight away Little Steve and I go to the ops tent, feeling our whole bodies levitate off the ground without the weight, and get new ECM batteries for the next operation. Then, and only then do we make a beeline for the register to book our half hour time slot on the internet.
I must update my Facebook status.

PB3 was one of four patrol bases along some important road in Babaji. It was just outside some small village, whose name I don't know. Further down the road we could see PB4, a low-lying profile in Hesco-beige colour. Our base was roughly the size of a football field, walled by Hesco. Accommodation tents were grouped at one end the cookhouse tent. On the other side were more tents for the gym, TV room, internet café, and ops room. In the middle was a big empty space which was the parking lot for when a unit with vehicles was garrisoning the base. There was a Piping Billy for hot water, and our dhobi was done in a brand-new orange cement mixer attached to a generator. Beside our tent, under a shelter was a huge stack of water bottles on a pallet, still wrapped in plastic.
We were given a tent to sleep in with a shelf made from Hesco offcuts. Lee and I went off to the only iso container. The chopper than brought us had also brought some fresh food, and we had had to run back and forth between the helicopter and the walls of the PB carrying boxes of powered milk, vegetables, cartons of eggs, meat and other fresh food. The HLS was outside the walls, on the other side of the road, guarded by kneeling soldiers manning a piquet line while the groceries was off loaded.
Everyone knew that "fresh" had come to the base. Fresh food was always preferable to rat packs, and it wasn't long before the quarter master was shouting "Fresh!" from the iso container. If you didn't get there soon, your team would miss out.
We came back laden with carboard boxes of shopping, and stacked tins of baked beans, fruit, broccoli, carrots, flour, vegetable oil, and all sorts of other food items that every soldier living on rat packs

would suddenly find exciting. The chef was away on leave, so each section took it turns to cook for themselves in the cookhouse tent. The unit we were helping out were the Coldstream Guards. They'd been conducting foot patrols to dominate the ground, and as usual had encountered problems involving IEDs. So they had patiently waited their turn for one of the twelve search teams in the brigade to come and help them out.

Half way through our tour. By now I was having sleeping problems. Some nights I'd be too terrified to sleep. I'd lie awake in the tent, or under the stars, looking up at them, thinking about what it's like not to be here. I'd listen to the others all sleeping, listening to the snoring, wondering how Smudge can drift off so suddenly. We'd all be lying in our camp cots having a chat, and he'd say something, and about ten seconds later, he'd be fast asleep.

But it wasn't the tent's snoring that that kept me awake. Death was such a regular occurrence, and it was by now quite clear to me that anyone can get killed, anywhere, and at any time. No one joins the army thinking about death. It's all about the adventure and challenge, to answer the question all young men have: do I have what it takes? Am I tough enough? For many, war is the ultimate challenge. An environment where two sides are trying to kill each other. But no one thinks it will happen to them. It's always going to happen to others, but not to you.

The first time this fact of military life hit me was on an exercise in Scotland. The OC gathered us all in a tent and announced that one of our barracks in Northern Ireland had been attacked, and two lads had been killed. It had been the day before they went to Afghan for their tour.

Often, I'd lie awake staring up at the stars. Occasionally a fighter plane would fly overhead. Then a few seconds later, there's his wingman. You can see their lights blinking against the night sky. They're going to be back in Kandahar tonight, in a couple of hours, safe in bed I'm thinking. When you not able to sleep at night when you have an early start in the morning, the more you think about how you can't sleep and how much sleep you're missing out on, the more you get agitated, the more awake you feel, even though you're really tired and have been looking forward to sleeping all day. Other nights, I would be able to get to sleep. But if I woke up during the night, that would be all the sleep I'd be getting. I would lie awake, unable to get to sleep again until dawn.

Maybe later, towards midnight or one in the morning, I'd finally drift off. And a few hours after that, around the time those two planes had finished their patrol, landed and shut down, we're being quietly woken up by whispers and nudges.

After Doug's death, I wrote a letter to my girlfriend. I then managed to book the sat phone and called her best friend in the UK. I told her about the envelope I was sending Anna, sealed inside another envelope I would post to her friend.

"If I get killed, could you please send the letter on to Anna?" I asked.

"Woah!" she exclaimed.

"Sorry…I know it's very unusual. Could I get your address?"

Behind me, the mortar platoon was preparing to fire and I didn't want to alarm anyone back home by the sound of firing, so after some awkward chit chat, we said goodbye to each other.

"Thanks for all you're doing!" I heard her say before we hung up.

The letter went with the post sack on the next helicopter. Becky received the letter a few days later, but fortunately never had to give it to my girlfriend. She gave it back to me after our tour was over and now lives in an old ammo tin in the loft with all the other letters, journal and log book.

We're searching a wall that had been used a lot by the infantry when on their patrols. It wasn't long before the Choghees buried IEDs in ten-meter intervals along the wall, which was the spacing the infantry kept to when they used it for cover. Luckily, a local shopkeeper had tipped us off about it. They didn't want IEDs in their area because it was bad for business.

Troopie had detailed me to search the corner while the others fanned out the other way. I slowly sweep the Vallon in a wide stretch at the bottom of the wall, and then turn it sideways to sweep the wall itself. When I was satisfied the ground by my feet was ok, I put the Vallon down behind me and got on my knees with the hand-held Hoodlum, and carefully hovered that into various nooks and crannies at the base of the wall.

Still nothing.

"Sapper Williams, are you done?" calls out Troopie from the ICP.
"Yeah, there's nothing here" I reply, standing up and shrugging my body armor with a little hop. I turn again to the wall and was about to take my customary step onto the searched ground when I had a sudden feeling of what I can only describe as dread, together with a very strong urge to not step on the ground. I had already checked it twice, with the Vallon and then the Hoodlum and neither have off any hits. But I didn't care. It was an urge that came out of nowhere. Don't step. Check again.
Very carefully, on my knees, I take off my glove and slowly brush the earth in a sideways motion towards me. A fingertip search is the surest way of knowing if something is there or not. Almost immediately, I uncover a length of twin flex. It was linked with a carbon rod pressure plate which would give off no magnetic signature. The charge was on the other side of the wall.
Later, in the middle of the field, the ATO detonated the three devices we had found. We watched the big explosion burst out of the ground, and then began the long trudge through the mud back to camp.
We arrive at dusk.

All of the tasks done at PB3 were foot patrols. Each task in the surrounding area involved waking up at about three o'clock in the morning to leave the wire at about four so that we were still well under way to our destination before the dicker screen could be set up.
A lot of these patrols were long, uneventful affairs with nothing more than stumbling around in the darkness for hours and keeping as quiet as possible. The lead man would always navigate a random, unpredictable path cross country. In this way, it would be almost impossible for the Chohgees to guess where we would walk.
Every now and then the whole multiple would pause while the map was being checked, with each man kneeling left and right in silence.
A pat on the shoulder would signal to move on again.
I had just stumbled forward to discover what the latest pause was. There was a large irrigation canal the patrol had been crossing. Big Steve was in front of me, and there were only about three other men behind. Big Steve made his crossing, and I entered the icy water which came up to my thighs. As I struggled up the opposite bank, he turned to give me a hand up. I turned to help the man behind me, and

turned back to find Big Steve still standing there a few paces away. He was not moving. I walked over to him and whispered, "what's the matter Steve?"
"Where the fuck are they?" he whispered hoarsely back. "They've left us."
In front of us, we could see absolutely nothing. We did not know if the multiple had gone to our left, or the right. The three others came over and joined us, standing in the dark.
"Oh fuck" someone breathed out quietly, realizing what had happened.
Getting lost on a night patrol can be done easily and happens on exercise all the time. Good soldiers remove all kit that rattles and dulls out anything that may shine. Equipment that has the 'on' confirmation light is taped up, leaving no noise or lights. For sneaking around at night, it is ideal. But if you get separated from your patrol, the stealth works against you. Getting separated from your comrades is probably one of the worst fears soldiers have in combat.
They could not have been very far away, but we could not see anything.
"Everyone, shut up and listen," whispered Steve.
We stopped shuffling around and listened. We listened in silence for about a minute and then suddenly from the darkness to our left, we hear a low noise. It sounded like a boot scuffing the ground. Without any hesitation, we moved in that direction in file. The rest of them were only twenty or thirty meters further along, kneeling again as they waited to cross another canal.
Towards dawn, we showed up at our destination. It was yet another small compound, home of another family of farmers. Later that morning, we man stag positions while the commander of the patrol has a shura with the men of the family and the neighbours who had trickled in from the countryside.
All guerilla wars are really tug of wars for the civilian population. Each side tries to win their support by showing off. The idea is that if you are seen to be on the side that is going to win, they'll be on your side because no one wants to be supporting the losers. When the losers are not there anymore, they have big problems.
Our patrols were all about the tug of war. We sally out of our end of the AO, walk all night deep into the Taliban side of the AO, show up

at their commander's house and knock on his door. Look what we can do to them. Do you think they can knock on our door?
So, the Chohgees do the same with us. Both sides are keen to show off to the audience what they can do. Only they don't send out armored vehicles or choppers. A few of them creep up to our side at night and bury some IEDs on the routes we always take, or even right outside the front gate.
One of their IEDs were found by an infantry patrol in an alleyway of the hamlet just down the road from the PB. It was an anti-vehicle land mine, rigged as an RC[11] device. The circular object, about the size of a dinner tray and completely plastic, was only discovered because of the metal detonator. Off to one side, buried and covered with alley way rubbish was the cell phone.
At one end of the alley way was a small building, and in that building was a small hole conveniently knocked in the roof. That hole gave eyes on the entire length of the alleyway and was where a Chohgee had watched the lead soldier slowly sweeping his Vallon, gradually approaching the IED. He had tried to detonate it, only to find no response. The ECM carried throughout the patrol had enclosed everyone in an invisible bubble, blocking all signals from reaching a device that they were stood over. He must have watched the soldier with the Vallon finally reach the buried bomb, stop and hover the metal detector over it several times in small sweeps. Then kneel in front of it (no one ever laid down just to investigate, despite the training) and fumble around in the dirt before turning to the man behind him. Find.
Troopie was pissed off when he learnt it was an alleyway. Alleyways are very dangerous. There are only two ways to go: forward or backward, plus the enemy has a pretty good chance of knowing where the boots will tread. He had told us about the find the night before in the tent.
"Why were they patrolling down the alleyway?" someone had asked. "There are other routes they could have taken."
His answer was veiled, as if unwilling to reveal the full dynamics of the O Group "We've had a chat about that," he said. "One thing I'd

[11] Remote controlled. An RC IED would have someone watching where the bomb was buried. When the victim walked beside it, it was detonated by remote control, usually a cell phone.

like to do during our stay here is some more barma training for the infantry. They want us to search the whole thing, to see if there's anything else down there."

The next day we began our search. We found nothing and achieved nothing apart from getting human shit on our gloves from carefully sifting through suspicious looking rubbish. The Taliban would do anything to dissuade us from searching too thoroughly. I think sometimes they did it just for the hell of it.

We had collapsed back to the ICP where we were chatting with the new IEDD team. The new ATO seemed too keen for his team. He had actually been trying to get them all to Sangin so that he could tick that box and say he had been to Sangin. We had our opinions about that idea, and so did his team. But he was a Captain, so we said nothing. The 2ic was a blonde woman from London, named Olive. I don't recall much about the infantry escort, apart from that he didn't seem very bright.

Search teams are always paired up with a four-man IEDD team. The search team finds them. The IEDD team destroys or dismantles them. The key people in a search team are the four searchers. The key person in the IEDD team is the ATO. Ammunition Technician Officer.

It would have been nice to keep the two teams together throughout the tour, but this never happened. We were always getting bumped around the place, and so were the IEDD teams. This could be a bad thing, because we got on quite well with some ATOs and their guys. Jim was a decent chap. So was Doug and the Scottish Guy and Captain Dangerous who we had later. But this ATO was a bit different, and made us see the benefit of swapping teams around from time to time.

I'm standing next to the tangeeman, trying to practice Pashtun phrases I'd picked up. He was a friendly guy from another part of Afghanistan. He was equipped with a Kevlar jacket and helmet which they were all required to wear, and a walkie talkie he held out in front of him.

The radio chattered into life as it picked up the comms between two enemy groups who had apparently been watching our activity all morning. We knew they were around because the locals were gone. But they were keeping their distance, relying on their IEDs.

The tangeeman laughs, "you know what they call you Britishers?"
"What?" I ask.
"They are calling you the mules."
"Mules? Why mules?" though I thought I knew the answer.
"Because you are always carrying so much on your backs, just like a mule."
We had heard this before and thought it was hilarious. The Gurkhas had a better name: The Monsters, because they had a reputation of beheading Taliban. One story circulating around at the time was of a Gurkha call sign who had finally captured the commander they were after. Unfortunately, he had been killed in the contact. They couldn't drag his body back when rounds are flying all over the place but they had to prove to the local population that he was dead. So, the section commander came up with the obvious solution. They cut off his head, stuffed it into a patrol pack, and bugged out. The story goes that they heard the enemy on the radio, something like: "Shit! The Monsters are cutting off heads!"
Two things happened as a result. The area suddenly went quiet for two weeks afterwards. And the Gurkha commander was sent back to the UK for some sort of psychological analysis.
The tangeeman listens some more to the radio chatter and translated, "they are saying that the mules are sitting down along the wall having a rest."
Behind me, our team was strung out sitting against the wall.
There's more talking, but the tangeeman can't understand it. He had recorded it and played it back to us. It was Arabic. I had picked up a bit of Arabic when I lived in Kuwait, but the only word I could make out was *khalas*. To finish.
"I think he's asking if we are finished."
The ATO walks by holding the big landmine, as we get to our feet and prepare to collapse back to the patrol base. "This'll make a hell of a bang," he says. He was going to blow it up in the field outside the walls.
Later that afternoon, we were stood down. We're not going out on the ground anymore and can relax until tonight's O Group, where we will be told what's happening tomorrow. I strip naked, grab a towel round my waist, flip flops and shower gel, and make my way out to where the showers are.
Like all the other showers in these outposts, they are nothing more

than off cuts of hesco wire fashioned into a cubicle. Hessian sacking provides the privacy, and a solar bag that's been left in the sun all day would provide five liters of warm water. You throw the suspension rope over a pole above your head, tie it off and it's all good to go.

I was just lathering up with soap and washing my hair when the air around me pounded my eardrums with a huge thunder clap, and my legs automatically gave way, letting my body fall to the ground. It was by far the loudest sound I had ever heard in my life.

I'm lying on the ground and for a fraction of a second, I didn't know what had happened. I quickly pat my naked body all over for any blood and look at my fingers. Only soap.

"Fuck sake!" someone nearby shouts. He was also on the ground. The ATO had detonated the landmine just beyond the wall. Normally they give warnings over the net so that no one panics. But word obviously didn't get to the showers, which were just on the other side of the hesco.

Explosions in war movies are nothing like the real thing. Nothing in war movies is like the real thing. After my tour, when I left the army, I went on a short training course in London. It was to teach people a few basic skills used in construction. Bricklaying, plastering and wiring. The class were all sat by their desks, wiring a plug. I was fiddling around with the braided copper and screwing the terminals tight when the tutor stoops over and shouts in my ear *"BOOM!"*

I jump in my seat. The whole class looks at us. The tutor laughs and announces "'E was finding bombs in Afghanistan!"

I was shocked at how long sudden loud noises could affect my mood. For days afterwards, I would be on edge. Even years later, it would still annoy me when my three-year-old son would jump around the corner, pointing a toy gun at me and shout 'bang!'

I would duck and then get angry and he would not know what he had done. But my wife would.

"Daddy doesn't like loud surprises" she says, ushering him safely out of the way.

One evening, Troopie comes into our tent after a chat on the sat phone.

"Gather round guys" he says with a smile on his face. "We're going on leave tomorrow".

A buzz is immediately injected into the tent. Everyone becomes like kids on Christmas Eve as we pack up to get out of here. True to their word, a Sea King comes for us the next morning to fly us to Bastion. We hand in our morphine and weapons, and are given flight instructions. At the check in counter, the squadron clerk gives us our phones but no one is allowed to turn them on yet.
And just like that, several hours later we are back in the UK.

I proposed to Anna on the Canary Warf platform. It was on her route home from the school she taught at. When she saw me waiting for her, she ran down the platform stairs and hugged me for a long time.
"Will you marry me?" I eventually whispered in her ear.
"Yes! Yes! Yes! Yes!"
Then a pause. "Wait a minute, you're not down on one knee!"
We both laughed, so I got down on a knee and proposed again.
The two weeks were over far too quickly. Anna and I went out to celebrate with Becky and her boyfriend. We went out to one of my favourite Walkabout bars in London, Temple Walkabout where I quickly got way too drunk. Everyone around me was living the normal life in a country I never would have guessed had been at war for seven or eight years. While waiting for the last tube in my intoxicated state, I became fixated on a poster in the Tube station advertising the latest online shooter game. There was a sleek looking character in the picture with a long beard, a reversed baseball cap and was wearing shades. Underneath it said 'this is the face the enemy fear'.
War is cool.

7
SANGIN
67 days remaining

We landed earlier than we were supposed to from R&R. We were in Sangin, the worst part of Helmand Province, technically on the last day of our leave. Everyone was absolutely livid with whoever's fault it was. Soldiers are allowed two weeks leave for six months of war, and this begins as soon as you leave the country, taking one of those days to fly back to the UK. Another precious day is spent flying back to Afghanistan.

Troopie had been separated from us. He'd gone to the USA for his leave and when the Army brought the dates forward, he got caught out. He'd been replaced with another guy as our RESA, a short ferocious-looking Scouser. We're a bit wary of the newcomer to the team, and everyone asks each other at discreet moments "so what do you think of the new guy?"

The Sea King drops off the team at Nolay, which is right next door to Sangin Central. It was on one end of the valley. A main road linked it up with Sangin, where FOB Jackson is just past the Y bend in the road. It's called the 611, and loads of soldiers have died or lost limbs trying to keep it open. At that moment, it was open.

From what I could make out, Nolay seemed to have once been some sort of leisure retreat place. There were lots of isolated buildings dotted around the place and what looked just like an empty cement swimming pool that no one had finished. The Army had taken over the buildings, and we followed an officer into one of them, to the ops room where he briefed us up on the new AO. We watched on a projector the digital feed of a camera fitted onto a toy plane that had flown the length of a road that they wanted opening. He paused the video every now and again, explaining certain features, distances, local behaviour. Route Onion, he said, was going to be very important in this area. I don't remember why it was important, because I wasn't really listening. What was important to me was that I was still supposed to be back in the UK, enjoying my last day of flushing toilets and singing the Eastender's theme tune with my fiancé. Our last day of leave in Sangin. No one wanted to be there. Everyone was already homesick.

Our team was going to be spending that night down in Jackson, and a convoy of Jackals was being arranged to take us down. Jackals are open-top vehicles, a bit like a massive rally car. There's a roll cage, and loads of machine guns, but that's about it. We managed to strap the mountain of kit we carry with us wherever there is space, hanging bergans off the side before finding some kind of hand hold or foot space for ourselves. I'm perched on the side of the vehicle, holding on with one hand, and with the other hand holding my rifle facing outwards. Our gunner turned out to be a South African, but he didn't really say much when I tried making any conversation with him apart from that he was from Cape Town. He seemed in a bad mood that he had been chosen to escort us on the twenty-minute drive down to Jackson.

The vehicles are all in line at the front gate, engines idling while some men on guard open up. As we slowly bounce along, the gunner turns to us and tells us what we should do if we get contacted.

"If we get ambushed, hold on because we'll be driving really fast out of it. If we stop, then jump off and get cover, but don't go off the road."

I nod, trying to make out like I've been through this a thousand times before and that I know what I'm doing. I'm nervous, but I'm also curious to see what Sangin was like. Everyone had heard about this town.

Slowly the convoy wound its way down the road, each vehicle loaded with men like baby scorpions on their mother's back, bristling with guns and looking out in all directions. The gunner keeps traversing his heavy machine gun down each alley at my back, and I'm keeping my rifle pointing down the alley ways we pass behind his back. Someone commented on how this is supposed to be our last day of leave, but generally no one is talking. I couldn't stop thinking, if the Taliban opened up on us now, they're bound to hit somebody. They can't miss. We're packed like sardines.

We passed some civilians, and as usual I waved at them as we drove by, but they just stopped and stared up at me from behind enormously long beards. I had no idea if I'm waving at Taliban, or waving at indifferent civilians who had just stopped caring about us. Before long, and for the first time since I had been in Afghanistan, we're driving on tarmac. It's also the first time I ever saw some kind of advertising. It was a huge bill board on the right side of the road, showing a smiling bearded Afghan man talking on the phone and gesticulating with his hands. He looks happy he is talking on that type of phone. Just after the bill board, we are driving through Sangin marketplace. Its bustling with people, on either side. The shops are like three sided buildings with the one side open up to customers, revealing a cavern of merchandise in each one. Some would be stacked with plastic products like washing baskets. Another would be farming shovels. Another would be empty except for a solitary sewing machine with an old man perched over it, peddling away.

Children squat down in groups here and there beside the drainage ditch, looking up at us, smiling and waving, and naturally, I'm trying my best to wave back at them while still holding on. Groups of adults lined the side of the road in small groups and paused from their work to stare up at us. I found it impossible to read their faces. FOB Jackson sits just off to the one side after a Y-junction. The other side leads away from the hub-bub of the market and eventually up to Inkerman. The shops straight away after the junction are all deserted. They're riddled with bullet holes and there are piles of human shit in each building. I found out later that the shop owners still had not returned to Sangin after the last spell of fighting between us and the Taliban.

Jackson is a lot more fortified than the other places we'd been to. Soldiers don't sleep in tents like in other areas, but in bunkers made of Hesco. Our bunker had just been vacated by the previous search team who had been given a moment's notice that they were going on their R&R. They left in a hurry.

As we settled into our new accommodation, we found a lot of their belongings that had been left which we later bagged up and put on board the next helicopter going to Bastion. In my bed space, I found what must have been that searcher's collection of things he had found while rummaging in the dirt: bullets, of all calibers.

Gibbs and I explored that evening. We discovered the shower system that had been erected by the river that ran through the camp. Enormous reservoirs of water were being constantly heated by small burners made by the engineers. These were connected by pipes that fed into six showers enclosed by a canvas barrier. Soldiers dressed in jumpers and with a towel around their waist were patiently waiting their turn, clutching their bag of soap and shampoo. A small group of

other men were hunched shoulder to shoulder, shaving in luke-warm water in their basins they had collected from the reservoirs.
So this was Sangin. We had heard so much about this place. It was the considered the worst area for British troops in Afghanistan, and about half of our casualties were from this one town. Since the famous siege back in the early days when a handful of heavily armed Paras beat back an overwhelming force of Taliban, the region had been held very shakily in our hands. The Taliban still had a very large unseen presence which tried hard to drive out our forces, or inflict heavy casualties on the occupying troops. The Army had established a series of major fortified strong holds throughout the valley, linked by a highway called the 611 which we had driven down earlier that day. The length of this road was dotted with small garrisons of men in patrol bases - platoon houses - whenever the infantry had occupied a house. As in other areas, it was their job to keep the road open by preventing the Chohgees from burying IEDs on it. The men in these patrol bases were close knit teams of infantry occupying compounds with key gun positions. The Taliban in Sangin were very good at laying IEDs and had become very daring. Some devices had been found just a few meters from the front gate of some bases. We had heard of one patrol base once being effectively cut off by IEDs, with the men inside being resupplied by other soldiers throwing rations over the walls.
At night, the activity would increase. Infantry patrols would leave the safety of their bases and head off into the darkness, carefully following the single man at the head of the column with the metal detector and keeping their eyes open for Taliban, who would also be taking advantage of the dark to bury new IEDs.
Although many IEDs had exploded along the 611, the highway had been more or less kept open, but only in certain parts. Leaving the road into the maze of alleyways and compounds on either side was playing with your life, but at that moment in time I was not fully aware of the new situation we had landed in. All I knew of Sangin was that it was supposed to be the most dangerous place in Helmand, and that Smudge, the only man in our team who had fought in Afghanistan before, had a more reluctant attitude about this place than the rest of us.
From across the valley, maybe a kilometer away, small arms fire chattered into life. The area seemed to rarely have quiet moments. It

was one of the first things we noticed when we arrived in Jackson. There always seemed to be shooting here and there. Some was distant, some was a lot nearer and occasionally you could hear overspill as rounds flew overhead. When I had first gone out on the ground, I remember being fascinated by the sound of shooting. Now neither of us of really noticed anymore. It had become a background noise. The contact that had erupted during our exploration of the camp grabbed a few soldier's attention because of the initial ferocity. Some would stop shaving as interest in what was going on slowly took hold.

"Woooo-eeee", a massive Jamaican soldier exclaimed as he paused from his laundry and stood up. "Some people over there are really getting fucked up!" he said in a thick Caribbean accent, smiling as he shook his head slowly and carried on with his hand-washing.

Over to one side of the panoramic view of the Sangin valley was the river. It was a very wide wadi with pebbles and had water flowing through it in several channels. Across one of the deeper, wider parts was the local ferry. It was a flat-bottomed boat that was being pulled across with local passengers huddled together on board. Other people were standing on the bank which it had just left and waiting for the ferry to return for them, oblivious of the noise of machine guns echoing across the valley.

BEEEEEEEEEEOWWWW! BEEEEEEEEEEOWWWW!

The residents of Sangin, like most of Helmand, had resigned themselves to this kind of life. There was not much they could do about it. First the Soviets, then each other, then the Taliban, then the Americans, and now us.

The fear returned that night in my doss bag. My kit was all ready to go beside me. My pistol and rifle cleaned and oiled. In pitch darkness of the COB, I felt alone with my fears. Tomorrow we'd be going out on the ground in this infamous Sangin, and I was desperately frightened. I can remember trying to pray, but no words came out. There was an IED that had been found by the ANA along a track in the dried wadi that ran through town. They wanted us to remove it, and search the area for more just to be sure.

The nervousness was still there at five in the morning, when we got up, and then at six, when we were eating breakfast. It was still there at six-thirty when we were waiting around for orders to get in the Teller and leave with the escorting Mastiff, and still there when we

left the 611 and drove down into the wadi.
It was a grey day. The infantry cordon had been in place a while now before we arrived, and were keeping a watchful eye out for the Taliban. The commander of the infantry was up ahead, discussing the bomb the ANA had found with our new RESA. Beside them was the ATO, who would be the man who would actually remove it, or blow it up. Lee and Steve were having a chat behind me, but I was straining my ears to hear what the commander was saying.
"...RC device...."
"...ANA patrol....."
"....we'll get your lads to search for more afterwards...." That made my heart sink. I still somehow had hope that we wouldn't have to leave unsearched ground that day.
Before the ATO could go near the device, we had to first check for wires connecting it with any hidden Taliban watching in the distance. The search team set out on a random path, giving the hidden bomb a long, wide berth with Little Steve leading the way with his Vallon and the rest of us following in his footprints. Buildings on each side were occupied by Afghan soldiers, who could be seen scanning our surroundings with binoculars.
It took an hour to walk a complete circle around the device and return to where we had started from. There was nothing leading in, so the ATO was safe to start his work. When he finally came back, people had gathered in the distance with semi-interest, just like people back home might be mildly fascinated with a small firework display. The resulting explosion was small in comparison.

6/2/2010 sangin
This morning's op had an ANA guy have his legs blown off. MERT came under fire trying to get him. Another guy was shot in leg.

Have a new wiz guy who didn't make such a good impression this morning. We were standing around, on standby when for some reason he comments: 'All the other REST teams I've been with have been blown up.'
Someone told him to shut the hell up.
Yesterday we had a 10-liner in wadi by airport lounge. RC device, 5kg that ANA had seen being buried the previous night. We blew it up in situ. Sangin seems to be more intense than other places we've

been to. There's always shooting, here, there...everywhere. There's loads of Taliban, and they've even had devices buried like 20m from the front gate, when guys would crawl along dead ground.
Like every other place, when we're not out on the ground, there's nothing to do except watch TV, read, or gym.

This time last week, Anna and I were on the train to Portsmouth.

7/2/2010
Caught the doc checking me out in the Mastiff today. She's good looking.

Our days in Sangin seemed to blend together in my memory. Some nights we slept at Jackson, other times in Nolay. Others would be spent holed up in a platoon house along the main road. The team was at the infantry commander's disposal, and they seemed to want all the stretches of Sangin to be searched at once. The Scouse would tell us each afternoon after he had been to the O Group with the senior commanders, and then let us know what the plan was for the next day, or the next few days.
We spent a few days concentrating on this famous Route Onion which some Major had briefed us about on our arrival, the same day no one had really been listening because everyone was still so angry at being brought back to war a day early. Before tackling the actual road, we first had to secure the surrounding houses, and that meant carefully climbing up ladders to get over the towering walls. Little Steve would always be the first to go up, peering over carefully down inside, then after being convinced no one was lurking inside, the second ladder would be passed up to him and he would carefully lower it down into the compound before climbing down, being careful to first search the ground around the ladder before he stepped onto the earth. Wearing body armour, helmet, carrying ammunition, water, his search equipment and having his swinging rifle constantly banging into him whilst maneuvering the ladder and carefully searching for bombs, it was a painstakingly awkward job. The man behind him was already at the top of the ladder, keeping an eye out over the wall while the rest of us waited patiently in a long spaced-out line, kneeling outwards, feeling the tight straps digging into the back of your bent knees.

The three soldiers carrying ECM, of whom I was one, had a nervous task of balancing at the top of a shaky ladder, judging the right moment to throw one leg over the wall and blindly try to locate the opposite ladder, listening to the others below you shouting up directions. "Left a bit! Lower…you're almost there, just move your foot down a bit more," they'd say. When you're perched on top of walls more than twice your height, carrying twenty or thirty kilograms on your shoulders, you can really feel how top heavy you are. Smudge would always be ahead of me in these wall scaling dramas. I would stand at the bottom of the ladder, trying to keep it steady while watching him at the top, standing completely still, waiting for the ladder to stop shaking and right moment to swing his leg over. Then he would disappear over the lip of the wall, followed by a burst of angry swearing.

The road itself was only wide enough for one vehicle, but mostly used by pedestrians or motorbikes. Each time anyone came down our way, we would stop them a good distance away. The locals knew the drill, and sometimes even before we signaled, they would lift up their long robes to show their naked abdomen and then turn around slowly for us to have a close-up view through our SUSATs for any suicide vests. Then one of us would motion to roll back each sleeve, and each trouser leg. Only then would that man be allowed to come forward, walking through us, smiling, and Smudge would always make sure he was greeted in Pashtu and smiled back.

"Salaam alikum"

"Alikum salaam."

"Manana." Thank you.

Then the man would walk away and carry on with his life.

There were a few Americans in Sangin. Sometimes we had a team of snipers looking after us as we slowly searched Onion, to add to the men watching us from the tall building overlooking the landscape. We'd been up to the top of the building before we began the search for us to have a rough idea of to what point we could be covered by them. That was how I knew the Grumpy South African guy was behind the machine gun up there. Everywhere we had been in Afghanistan, there seemed to be a small network of the South African mafia. Because of my childhood spent in Southern Africa, I would always find myself discovering these small groups in patrol bases and check points. Once they knew where I had grown up, I'd always be invited for a brew and talk about Joburg, and Pretoria, and how things were in SA these days. The fact that Grumpy South African guy was still not communicating bothered me at first, until I reasoned he might be Afrikaans.

We didn't find much on that route. The surprise and speed with which the commanders wanted to secure the road worked – the Taliban had no idea, and had not had time to dig in any IEDs. Behind us, the sappers, who are found all over Helmand, began unloading pre-cut timber and other building material from a quad-bike and trailer. They had been waiting for us to make sure the ditch they would be working on was cleared of IEDs before they began making a bridge over it. Behind us began the sound of carpentry, hammers banging away, and the noise of sawing. By the end of the day, a small bridge would have appeared in a previously random crossing point, linking up an isolated patrol base with the main supply route. The engineers proceeded over the next few days to block up each culvert we searched with obstacles to prevent anyone from placing a bomb underneath.

Only Gibbs found something. It was a coil of thin copper wire which had once been an alternator from an engine, and it was in an irrigation ditch. An unraveled alternator was often used as a command wire. Whoever had crawled along the ditch at night to place a bomb under the nearby culvert had probably abandoned the idea when he found his command wire in such a knot.

We're in a small platoon house for the night. It's one of the outposts strung out over the length of the 611. It's a three-story house, made of concrete, not mud. It seems like the owners were wealthier than their rural counterparts in other parts of Afghan. A small group of infantry had occupied the house, keeping turns at staying alert. There were machine guns on the rooftop, which had a good view of the surroundings in all directions. Each one of us had visited their toilet – a camping chair with a hole cut out of the seat, inside a separate room from the house. A yellow bucket was placed underneath the chair, and that's where you put your wag-bag in. There was no lock on the door which led to a few accidental intrusions, but no one cared about that kind of stuff anymore. It was a nice place to have some time to yourself for a few minutes.

We had decided to call it a day and come back to this compound where we would be spending the night, before going out the next day to search more of that road. Overnight it was being carefully watched by our snipers, together with the American team who were helping us out. Until then, we could relax. The petty rules and regulations we had found with other regiments, even in a war, did not seem to apply to the Rifles. They seemed to recognize that soldiers have more to worry about than haircuts and sideburns and which color boots matched which color battle dress. We lay sprawled out, soaking up the last rays of the sun. By undoing your body armor and laying it upside down, you can lie on it like a sort of mattress, and that's what everyone was doing. Gibbs, Lee and Little Steve were all playing with a small bouncy ball on the bricked-up ground. Someone had brought out their i-pod and speakers, which were on their improvised table, and a couple of us had scrolled through the list of available songs and had booked an unofficial queue of tracks they wanted to hear. At the moment, *The Ting Tings* was blaring out.

From the top of the roof, the machine gunner began firing. Its very loud, and suddenly everyone jolts up, grabbing weapons and body armor. The infantry all around us are yelling, "Stand to! Stand to!" and running indoors. "Stand to!" I'm shouting, struggling with my helmet strap. I already had my body armor on and grabbed my rifle, sprinting up the stairs two at a time with the others. More machine gun firing, a long, long burst. By the time we got to the top and fanned out across the roof, I was breathing hard. We flung ourselves against the wall, rifles pointing out in all directions, looking for targets. Where were they? What was happening?

"You see anything?" asked the rifleman next to me.

"No."

We're both looking through our SUSATS, trying to hear what the machine gunner was saying to the sergeant, who was crouched next to him, looking through his telescopic sights on his rifle. On the one side of the house, the surrounding neighborhood dropped away in a gentle slope towards the valley's river. On the other side, the terrain sloped upwards into empty brown land. We were located right at the outskirts of town, and the only other building up the slope was an old shot-up compound wall which had once been a house of some sort. That's where the Taliban which the gunner had spotted lay dying. He had been seen making stealthy progress towards us, when the gunner noticed he wasn't paying any more attention to the herd of goats that had by now run off. When the soldier saw the Afghan running towards the compound, he opened fire.

"I'm sure I got him," the man was saying. He was another South African. "He's right there, by that hole." That didn't seem to make any difference to his sergeant, who was angry at the long burst of firing we had all heard. When he saw that there still was no movement, he turned on the gunner.

"What the fuck was that?!" he shouted, hitting the man on the helmet. "You fire short bursts. Three to five rounds. How do you expect to hit *anything* shooting like that?"

We stayed on the rooftop for another fifteen or twenty minutes. There still was no movement from the compound wall. Maybe the gunner had killed him after all. I still had *The Ting Tings* in my head, playing it mentally to pass the time while trying to see through the scope where the body was supposed to be.

I'll miss the catch if you throw me the ball,
I'm the last chick standing up against the wall...

The Taliban in Sangin had taken advantage of the urban surroundings by getting as close as they could to a particular compound where they knew British soldiers had occupied. They would give their best stone-throwers hand grenades to lob as far as they could, hoping to clear the wall and explode among the unsuspecting men inside.

After the excitement had subsided, I got talking with the man next to me. He told me all about this grenade throwing activity, and about the town itself, the details of a few specific contacts they'd had, and that he had lost five friends in four months. He also answered a question I had had about Sangin since we got there.

"That screaming every night," I asked. "The howling. Do you guys hear it?"

"Yeah, sometimes."

"What *is* it?" On some nights, we could hear strange sounds coming from all around town. It sounded like a pack of dogs howling at the moon, but at the same time, it sounded far more like humans than dogs. It was weird. So far, no one in the team had been

able to place it.
"Oh, that's them," he explained. "I think they're trying to scare us."
Just then the sergeant spoke up, addressing everyone crouched behind the walls. "That's it lads." He left the man behind the machine gun with one other to carry on watching the building before heading back down through the doorway. "Remember your weapon states," he added. We followed behind, one after the other, making our weapons safe again.
When we got down, someone had insisted on replaying the *Ting Tings* song that had been interrupted earlier.

That's not my name...(dum-dum)...that's not my name...(dum-dum)...that's not my name...(dum-dum)...that's not my....name.

It was like nothing had happened.
The rest of the evening remained relaxed. We filled up the improvised couches surrounding the table, listening to Bob Marley, Led Zeppelin and ACDC, talking about an article someone had read in the *Nuts* magazine, or girlfriend situations back home, with each person giving their expert advice on what to say in the next Facebook session. We'd all taken turns at cooking our rations in the kitchen inside the darkened house by head torch, and everyone was busy eating and talking.
The Scouse had had an angry word on the phone to some commander in the main FOB half a mile away over some phantom magazines on another stretch of road which was not necessarily our main effort. The road should have otherwise been searched by an infantry barma team, because it was not deemed to be high risk. However, once it was mentioned that there were some SA80 rifle magazines seen lying there all by themselves, the suspicion and threat level escalated. Suddenly having a search team clear the road seemed justifiable after all. We had searched that small stretch earlier that afternoon, finding neither magazines, nor any IEDs. We couldn't help but wonder if there had been any magazines there at all, and that as long as they had us, they wanted to use us to search everything, instead of high-risk areas.
The next day at first light, when we set off back to tackle the remainder of the road, we walked past a large patch of blood on the

ground. No one really cared enough to ask what had happened.

We're on another isolation on the side of the 611. There was a bit of road that was in some dead ground because of a bend, so the stag position up at Inkerman had not got eyes on it. It was only a stretch of about fifty metres. We started off isolating it from any command wires running in from the alleyways on either side. It was a really cold day, and the wind was blowing hard.

We were making progress down the right side of the road, first Little Steve as the pathfinder, then Smudge, then Gibbs, then myself, the ATO, and the others behind. As we're crossing each alleyway opening, each soldier had to wait until the man behind is on the corner to give cover before he crossed, so if anyone did pop out, there were at least two rifles pointing back.

Gibbs, our cable-detector man was hooking each alley way as he crossed them. Alleyways are often used to lay a command wire. They open up onto the road where an IED is buried, and the wire will be buried all the way off the road, through the alleyway to a firing point where some Chohgee is watching vehicles go by. So, when we cross the mouth of the alleyway, we have to scrape the ground with a metal hook, digging right in. If there is a wire buried, you'd rake it up. Because I'm the man behind Gibbs, I'm covering the alleyway as he crosses it, hooking as he goes. He put the hook down on the ground by our feet and straight away, we both heard a dull *phuk.* We look at each other and together look down at the earth. Right where he had started hooking the ground, we saw a bit of uncovered white plastic showing through the dirt. He'd put down the hook right on top of a pressure plate. Fortunately, he had not done it hard enough to detonate it. He would have been blown up, and I would have at least have lost my legs. All that was needed was a little more force.

"What are you two gawping at?" asked our ATO, inquiring about the hold up in his thick Scottish accent.

"Er, find" answered Gibbs, as if he just dropped a glass, and, still in surprise, didn't quite know what to do just yet. The ATO came up to us and peered over my shoulder to the two inches of white surface Gibbs had uncovered.

"Yeah, that's a ten-liner…we'll be leaving that one," he says. "It ain't on the road. Make sure you mark it." He turned to the others

strung out behind him to let them know there was a marked IED up ahead on the left, by the corner of the wall.
It was only much, much later that I really thought about how close we had both come to losing our lives. At the time, I had forgotten about it within a few minutes.
Further up the road, we spotted the kid, all by himself. He was by a petrol station, the only one I had seen in Afghanistan, and he was sitting on his haunches. He was about nine or ten. We had seen him from a distance away, and behind us, the gunner in the escorting Mastiff had tried firing mini-flares in his direction to warn him to move away. Initially, he wandered off, but afterwards he reappeared, and took up the same position again, huddling himself against the cold.
Smudge was speaking to the Scouse with his radio-headset.
"We're being dicked," he said, then paused. "Roger," and then motioned for the rest of us to carry on. No kid would be out here on such a cold day unless someone had sent him.
As we got nearer, we shouted at him to go home.
"*Khadanark!" Danger!* we shouted. "Go!"
He stayed.
Smudge and I pointed our rifles at him, bellowing, "*GO HOME!"* in English. He got the message. We didn't see him after that.
Dickers had always been a problem with regard to the rules of engagement. The question of whether or not we could kill civilians watching and reporting our movements to Taliban had been highly controversial. Sometime during our tour, the rules had changed – we were allowed to kill dickers. It made no difference to us what senior commanders or MoD officials had decided. We weren't going to kill children, even if they were telling the Taliban everything we did.
Later on, we began working at searching the road itself, feeling the cold wind rush past us, blowing trees from side to side. As usual, I'm on the left in front, and on the other side of the road is Little Steve. Everyone is trying to forget the cold and instead concentrate on the ground immediately in front of our feet.
"Check it out," said Little Steve. I looked at him to see what he was looking at. A local man was walking down the side of the road away from us, along a wall. The thing which caught Steve's attention was how close he was walking to the wall. He was walking calmly, but specifically with one foot behind the other, deliberately keeping to a

narrow route. He was also so close to the wall that he was brushing past the surface.
"Great," I said. "That's just what I like to see."
Not long after that, right after I had got my boots soaking wet searching a long puddle in the road, someone, from somewhere in the surrounding buildings began shooting at us. I spun around, and on my way to the ground I remember seeing Big Steve and Smudge spinning around diving for cover behind the Mastiff. There was a long burst of automatic fire, then the Mastiff gunner behind the machine gun opened up and that's when Lee and Gibbs both got up and sprinted back towards the armored vehicle, zigzagging, bent double and carrying all their kit. Next, I found I had lifted myself off the ground and was sprinting, low, zigzagging and moving extremely fast. I didn't even know I was doing it. Little Steve was right behind me, and we all crouched huddled beside the Mastiff, trying to work out where the shooting was coming from, listening to the soldier above us return fire with the gimpy.
There was a loud *claaaang!* just above our heads, and then another, followed by a shrill *piiinnnng!* We all looked above us in wonder at these strange noises before the realization seemed to come upon each of us at once. *We're on the wrong side!*
"Fuck!" someone swore.
I don't think I've ever seen people move from a stationary, crouching position so fast. We stampeded around the Mastiff to the other side, clawing each other to get to safety first, while one or two crawled underneath. By the time we were safe, however, all the shooting had stopped. Everyone was laughing at having ran to the wrong side of the Mastiff, assuming the shooting had come from the river side.
"Those Chohgees must have been pissin' themselves laughing at us," said Big Steve, "No wonder they couldn't hit anything."
"They were too excited," remarked the ATO. "All that happened was they got over-excited and began shooting before they all ran away when he began shooting back," he said, looking up at the gunner.
Like all other contacts, everything had happened so fast and suddenly I had no time to figure out who was shooting, or if it was at me, or where they were. The road we had just ran down looked just like it had before. Absolutely nothing had changed. Once again, they had hidden in concealed positions, watched as four slow moving

targets walked along the road, giving the ground most of their attention – and they'd all missed, before running back to whomever had sent them to kill us. I still had no clue where they had been hiding.

We slept that night on top of a knoll along the 611, called PB Blenheim. The hill, surrounded by a wall of Hesco was home of yet another small group of infantry making a living as best they could, whilst guarding the road which ran past below them. Our two Teller's which we had been driving around Sangin, had trouble getting up the slope. Little Steve and myself were standing top cover, back-to-back, with rifles pointing outwards like pee-shooters. We were trying not to stand on anyone down below, but it was hard to keep footing and get knocked around. The Teller's vehicles spun in the mud as the tires struggled to gain traction, and slowly the vehicle pulled itself to the top. Everyone congratulated Lee before clambering out and seeing the new place we would be spending the night. There was what looked like a shanty town. It could only be described as a very large tee-pee, made up of corrugated metal, sheets of plastic, tent canvas, Hesco, and iso-containers. Inside revealed evidence of a tightly-packed community. Camp beds lined the walls amidst piles of personal kit through which pathways had been kept open to walk. Candle wax dripped down among the mud floor, and there was a smell of damp, unwashed laundry. It was icy cold.

Everyone looked around for somewhere to dump his kit and a place to sleep. No one wanted to sleep in the mud, but there weren't enough beds to go around. A few of us opted to somehow sleep in the Tellers. After careful consideration, Big Steve decided the iso container would be a good idea. He later admitted it was one of the coldest nights of his life.

A few of us found beds belonging to some soldiers who would be on a patrol that night. They let us sleep in them while they were gone. After we had secured our sleeping arrangements, we had a quick look around, but the patrol base was so small, there was nothing much to see. Just more sangars with heavy machine guns or grenade machine guns overlooking the valley. I remember then that for some reason, we posed for a team photo. I still have it with me, all of looking at the camera. I think the reason why I remember that specific photograph is because of what happened next. The Scouse was away off by himself, on the sat phone. Then he came back. "Everyone, gather in the tent," he said. We all fell quiet, walking through the canvas flaps. By now we knew what this meant. Each time someone came back from a chat on the sat phone and told us all to gather round, it meant that someone had been killed. Who was it? we all wondered.

The Scouse spoke to the crowd again. "Earlier this afternoon, there was an incident involving an IED…the result is that Dave is KIA." A quiet gasp from everyone. Dave? Dead? I thought back to the last time I had seen him, when my mom was dying and he had helped me back at Bastion. No one knew any details. Just that he had been killed in an IED explosion.

The remaining memories of that evening are all cold and damp and grey. The wind that day had died down a bit, but had brought heavy, dramatic clouds which threatened rain. Once again, I couldn't sleep but instead spent two hours listening to the rain pouring down outside, beating on the tent canvas and hammering on the corrugated iron. Thinking about the last few times I had spent with Dave, replaying conversations in my head. A trickle of rain water had rapidly streamed down through the roof, following the bed netting above my head and had begun pouring like a tap onto my body, quickly soaking the bed-owner's woolen blankets and doss bag I had arranged myself in. In a fury, I beat uselessly up at the waterfall raining down on me before getting out of bed and being forced to fix the problem. It was about midnight, when the rain subsided a little. The mortars outside were firing into the night. Eventually I decided since I was awake, now was a good time to go to the toilet. Putting my boots on, and stumbling out of the entrance I was greeted with an amazing panoramic view of the whole valley. I can still see it now, as clear as yesterday.

The massive cotton-wool clouds were still there off to the right, towering high above the landscape, and they were being illuminated from time to time by the lightening within them, exposing deep shades of blue and grey. Off to the left, opposite the clouds, was a line of lume rounds hanging by their little parachutes. They were slowly descending diagonally down to earth, lighting up the ground below them. The mortars fired again and again, sending more up to take their place where the first had begun.

Standing on top of the hill, urinating into the desert rose, I took this all in. It was beautiful. I didn't know that the night patrol whose beds we were borrowing had been blown up, and that the mortar teams were firing a continuous barrage of lume to help the rest of the men in the patrol who were working furiously to save their two friends. In the morning, we woke up exchanging rain-water horror stories. Big Steve had almost frozen to death in the iso-container. Smudge had been sleeping peacefully underneath a building reservoir of rainwater. When the dam finally broke, it fell right onto his face. I tried not to laugh when I heard it, because it was clear he was in a foul mood.

Because we were being bumbled all over the place, our evenings were being divided between sleeping in relative comfort down at Jackson, or sleeping anywhere we could find space in the surrounding patrol bases. We soon began to forget about Camp Bastion – that desert paradise - and instead looked forward to the creature comforts of a semi-established Forward Operating Base. In our Hesco bunker, we had in a sense our own rooms, with each bed space partitioned off with blankets, or ponchos acting as a screen to give a sense of privacy. I even had a bit of Hesco-wire fashioned into a bedside table. In an area of the bunker, we had another low, wide table, serving as the common area. Every now and again during our free time one of us would produce a laptop, hooked up to the electricity supply and we'd spend an evening crouching over a tiny laptop screen, straining our ears at the pathetic sound and shooting angry looks at anyone who made too much noise when they entered. We'd sometimes buy drinks of Coke, Sprite or Fanta from the small Afghan shop which had been set up on camp. If I remember correctly, $10 would get a crate, and we'd all take turns to buy for everyone. Then someone else would produce some smuggled vodka, and we'd all pour a bit in.
I'd been working my way through *Generation Kill,* giving a mental commentary to myself exactly how much of it was realistic. One film in particular that had angered everyone had been *The Hurt Locker*, for how inaccurate everything was. I had spent my childhood growing up on these war films and fostering some sort of glorified view of war. Now I watched them with mild amusement. Nothing was like I had been taught in the movies.

There was the outside gym, though a lot of that was also improvised to an extent. Someone had made a heave bar, there were a few crash matts falling apart, and a variety of weights. There would always be soldiers there. Little Steve and Gibbs would naturally be gym buddies. They had their own specific programme they were busy sticking to each time we stayed the night in the FOB.
There were internet terminals - those vital personal links to the UK - comprised of the usual dusty laptops, and a few telephone booths to call home. Every soldier is given a phone card with a number to dial, reading from the card with one hand, and holding the phone against your ear with the other. Waiting for the click, and the silence. Then the woman's voice.
"Welcome to Paradigm services. Loose talk may put your comrades in danger..."
From there you had to listen to the following options she gave you, and finally she allowed you to punch in the number you wanted to dial.
Everyone had I think half an hour of phone-time added each week, but there was always the option to buy more minutes. One of the outrages I remember at the time was the discovery that prison inmates back in the UK were allowed more minutes each week than soldiers in a war. Whether this rumour was true or not, I never did find out.
My calls were usually made to my girlfriend, followed by a few minutes each saved to phone members of my family. Like my letters, I found it hard to know what to say. I didn't want to worry anyone, so there was a lot I chose to keep to myself. But that only meant that everything I could talk about was either boring or repetitive. I'd talk about the food, the weather, getting to sleep in sometimes, how cold it was. I had always imagined I would come back one day full of war stories, of how granddad did his bit in Afghan. Instead, I found I'd become extremely reluctant to discuss any actual combat-related topics, especially with family. Instead, these conversations would always end with the shopping list.
"What do you want us to send to you?" everyone would ask. The answer was always the same.
"Chocolate, beef jerky and wet-wipes. Especially the wet-wipes!"
Then I'd remind them of the most important thing of all. "Don't

forget to send letters! I mean actual written letters." I'd remind everyone of this several times in our phone conversations.
The supply helicopter frequenting these FOBs would always bring a sack of mail. When we ran out to help unload all the kit, it was always the most important item, the thing everyone was sub-consciously looking out for to ensure the chopper didn't fly off with it still onboard. It was the first thing that everyone in the camp asked about after the helicopter had left, and normalcy returned.
"Did it bring the mail?"
When the helicopter didn't bring any, everyone would be in a bad mood and blame every rear-echelon soldier in the supply chain who hadn't been left to live in some hole for six months. We'd blame the post-room clerks at Bastion whose job it was to distribute UK mail throughout the brigade to the C-IED taskforce. We'd blame the C-IED clerks whose job it was to get the mail onto the flight-line. We blamed everyone for a few moments, and then carried on with the day.
When it did bring mail, one of us would go off to the ops room to check the mail sacks to see if one wasn't labeled C-IED. When no such sack was found, the blaming would continue a while longer, and another day of waiting and hoping would pass until the next chopper came.
But if such a mail bag was found, it was like Christmas, especially if there was a backlog of two or three mail sacks. Once, after an exceptionally long delay, five sacks were delivered to our bunker. As soon as we saw them, everyone became both the best of friends and little children at the same time. One of us would empty a sack onto the table and read out the names on each letter, handing them out as he did so. This became a ritual. The parcels would be opened, to reveal all the pieces of home that were sent in them. The letters, called *blueys*, were ripped open where they had been sealed along the sides and bottom, and the room hushed down a little as people immediately began reading the opening lines. Some of the blueys would have photographs, and these would always end up stuck on the walls in some way besides each bed.
Those evenings when the post arrived were tremendous morale boosters. For some reason, getting an email and clicking on the inbox just didn't have the same impact as getting a stack of letters in the mail sack when the helicopter flew off.

The Taliban had just attacked us, and there were dead men lying on the ground before our sangar. One of them was wounded and propped up against a tree, facing away. I wanted to put him out of his misery so shot him in the head, but I missed slightly and hit the side. He screamed. I fired again, he screamed again. I got angry and switched to automatic and let loose a burst at him full into the back of his head. His screaming didn't stop, but grew louder, filling my ears.
I wake up.

A new Taliban IED team was in the area, or so they told us. They had been operating off the 611, around the Inkerman AO, and they must have been either new at the job or just sloppy because a couple of IEDs had been found that had failed to function. One was a directional focused device, pointing around the corner at the stag position at the front gate. When it was discovered, we found that the string which triggered it had been pulled. Whoever's turn on stag it was had been a lucky man.
Not so lucky for those Taliban though. After an explosion in the neighbouring alleyway, some soldiers went to investigate what it was. It had been an own goal. Four Taliban had been killed while burying another IED when it went off. Others had been struggling with two of the bodies before the infantry opened up on them. The other two dead bodies were left in the alleyway. Infantry had cordoned off the area from curious local passers-by who had stopped to watch.
"Fuck off!" shouted one soldier, who was killed the next day, waving his hands in wide sideways arcs. "Go on, piss off!" he yelled, throwing a clod of dried earth at them. The locals could have been anyone.
Two soldiers, one a woman, were at the entrance to the alleyway right before the T-junction, and the first thing everyone wanted to know was where were the dead Chohgees.
"Right round the corner," the woman said. "You can go take a look at 'em if you want".
The first thing that struck me was that they looked exactly the same as the locals we saw every day, like the cars full of men staring at the patrol as they drive past, or the farmers out in the fields. I would

never have been able to tell them apart. I thought about the interpreter in Nad-i-Ali who said he had recognized one of the Taliban running away and shot him, how the British soldiers just didn't see it. Always signs of Taliban, and finally Taliban.

One man had clearly been thrown against the wall of the alleyway before crumpling up. He was lying on his back, staring up at the sky with lazy, half-closed eyes and his legs doubled underneath him. I was taken aback at how lifeless his eyes were. One of his shins had been smashed in, and there was a hole large enough to see all the way through, making his calf twice as thick. There was another massive wound on his neck, which is probably what had killed him. I don't think I will ever forget how thick that lower leg was because of the hole. Flies were crawling on the meat.

The other man had been much closer to the explosion. The remains of his body were a huge mess. It was difficult to make anything out. One of the soldiers in the IEDD team had the horrible task of finding a finger and getting a finger print. Then it could be cross referenced with finger prints found at bomb-making factories. Maybe one of the dead men was the bomb maker.

That alleyway seemed so personal, like a crime scene. I felt like an intruder stumbling upon something that happens only in secret. Like a school boy who could be discovered breaking the rules at any moment. The corpses seemed so limp. Just like rag dolls, I thought to myself. I got the feeling that that alleyway belonged to them now.

"You see some shit around here you don't normally get to see," I told the woman on my way back. To this day, I'm still surprised at the way I said those words.

Those two dead Taliban didn't stay in that alleyway. Later, when the real nightmares began, they'd appear like long lost relatives, twisted and grotesque, with their lifeless eyes and ragdoll limbs.

A couple of Chohgees blew themselves up yesterday trying to lay an IED. We went up to exploit the bodies. It was in an alleyway. One had been thrown against the wall before crumpling in the corner with chunks ripped from him. Their wounds were unbelievable.

Four weeks left on the ground (?)

We're on another task. This one was just off patrol base Esre, a nearby compound. We were told about it the night before in the briefing. One of our men had been blown up on the corner of the wall during a foot patrol. It had turned out to be the same soldier I had seen the day before shouting at the Afghans to go away. The explosion had blown off both his legs, an arm, most of his torso, and his head, which no one could find. He'd been killed instantly. His helmet had been blown all the way into the patrol base, a few hundred meters away.

The medic we had assigned to us that morning was a very pretty Welsh girl. Gibbs had been the lucky one who had happened to sit next to her as we all clambered into our places in the Mastiff, and we were all secretly giving him the look, trying to make him feel self-conscious. The medic smiled away, not noticing, or pretending not to notice the effect she was having on Gibbs. He had just looked angrily away from Little Steve, who was grinning at him from the corner of his eyes, and locked his gaze on me instead. A smirk slowly broke across my face.

The gunner of the vehicle happened to be the Company Sergeant Major of one the infantry companies in Sangin. His poor driver, who must have been used to the tirade of abuse pouring through the net, did his best to steer the Mastiff as gently as he could, avoiding craters of previous explosions. It was difficult for him to see over the massive bonnet. Instead, the Sergeant Major was seeing for him.

"Left, Vinny, left...left! LEFT!" he screamed. The whole vehicle lurched like a ship about to capsize, then came right again. Everyone in the hull of the Mastiff regained their momentarily jarred vision, just in time to see that Gibbs had been thrown against the medic. More subtle grins. The medic, I suspected, had begun to notice what was going on.

"Vinny! Right! Slowly, SLOWLY! Vinny! VINNYYOUFUCKINGDICKISAIDSLOWLY!"

There was another violent jolt, but no one complained. Everyone was feeling sorry for Vinny, while at the same time marveling at the rage in the Sergeant Major's voice. This continued all the way until we arrived at our destination.

The main job for the day was to see if anything could be found out about the device that had killed this man. It meant clearing a path up to the explosion crater for the specialists to safely work in to take photos and gather any forensic information. On the isolation we all notice its very quiet. There's no one around in all directions, and that

is never a good sign. We cautiously entered a compound, everyone following behind the lead searcher. No one was home. The wind was kicking up the dust and making an abandoned cloth hanging in the gateway flap in the wind. One of the corners of the compound had collapsed from the explosion. The patrol had passed on the outside corner, each man unknowingly passing inches to the hidden danger, until one of them had trodden on the pressure plate. On the return we pass smaller bits of the victim - bits of flesh, bone, clothes, little components of a rifle, and the huge patch of blood where the stretcher was clearly outlined. We'd been given evidence bags and were picking up left over bits as we went along. I found a bit of his head, covered in ants, more bits of bone, pieces of meat. The man's platoon sergeant had come along with us, and as I picked them up, I would pass them back to him to put in his evidence bag. I noticed that the skin was really glossy, almost shiny and very white. They were easy to see because of the ants. Looking at the small parts of skull, I remember thinking, no wonder we never found his head.
When we arrived back in the compound where the infantry had been covering us, the ATO and a weapons specialist wanted to get down to the explosion crater, and only needed two searchers. Gibbs and Little Steve volunteered. I was supposed to stay in the compound with the bags with body pieces in, make sure none of the infantry have a peek. After covering the bags up as discreetly as I could, I lay on my back in the sun, looking up at the sky.
I have read of the feeling that soldiers sometimes get when something is about to go wrong, and I clearly remember suddenly getting it. It was a feeling of dread for about ten seconds, and I sat upright. I thought to myself, this day is not like the others. It was a clear bright day. After a few minutes I relaxed again, closed my eyes, feeling the sun on my skin.
There was an enormous bang.
Right in front of me, a jet of brown earth shoots high into the air. Everything happens in split seconds. Faces looking at each other in shock. I look at another soldier who is looking back at me, mouth open. In that split second there's silence, and then suddenly shouts and screams from everywhere. The next bits seem as if I was watching myself. Grabbing a Vallon, running past Lee, what the fuck is he doing? Vallon calibrating noises, running after the Scouse down to where the others are. They're all prone. As if it's someone

else I'm hearing myself shout where? Where? Where? Where? Everything is fast, happening at once. I didn't know what had happened. Someone's pointing at me, yelling. Get the fuck up there! I ran up, see a crater (not very deep) and remember running into it, thinking that it's safe ground.
Off to my right I see it all.
Oh fuck. Oh Jesus. Steve is walking slowly around Gibbs, searching around him, shouting at him, talking to him. "What are we going to do in the gym today? Stay with me!"
Gibbs is lying on his back. He had been thrown about five or ten metres. There are glimpses of white and red and brown. I'll never forget seeing him there like that. I throw Steve my tourniquet, and hop in big strides the last few metres to where Gibbs was thrown. From the corner of my eye, I see his metal detector. It's snapped in two. I remember wincing when I'm hopping to him. Half expected to get blown up too.
When I'm there, I'm shouting to the others to throw me their tourniquets. Smudge threw me some. Gibbs is making a very distressing noise when he is trying to breathe.
I knelt between his legs. This can't be happening. Where the fuck do I start? On my right, the leg ends at the knee, with the bone in sharp edges and his flesh is skinned all the way up to his groin. Chunks of flesh are missing and all the hair is burnt. I remember lifting it up and feeling the flesh come away from his femur, so I have to do it carefully as I put the tourniquet on and tighten it as hard as I could. Smudge was shouting behind me "well done buddy." They couldn't come until it was fully searched.
Gibbs's penis was gone, along with most of his abdomen. Instead, it was all a big red mess. I had no idea what to do. This can't be happening. This isn't happening.
Gibbs's other leg had been blown off neatly at the knee. His femur ended at the ball and socket joint and was sticking out on its own without any flesh. I lifted that leg up by the leg joint. It was so slippery and very white. Gibbs was sort of cuddling up to Steve. He was crying. I'll never forget that. Steve was getting a tourniquet on his arm, which was also gone.
This bit is a bit vague and I don't remember exactly what happened. I remember screaming for the medic because suddenly Gibbs stopped making his distressing breathing noise and went silent.

That's when I began screaming "MEDIC!! MEEEDDDDICCCC!! *GETTHATFUCKINGMEDICHERENOW!"*
It seemed like ages. Two medics came sprinting in with their kit, ragged breathing. One was crying, but they immediately began doing their job, putting drips in and talking to him and getting more field dressings on. Jodi was talking to him, "Hello darling" and then asked if he could spit, and I could see him trying to do so. Tubes went into his arm, and another needle into his chest with a tube connected to a bag of fluid. She gave it to me to hold up and squeeze. Everything was happening fast, and in a blur. At another stage I was saying to the other medic as deliberately and calmly as possible "tell me what to do...tell me what to do...what do you want me to do?" and she helped me get some kind of strap around his pelvis and tighten it. The signaler is there sending the 9-liner to Bastion, and asked how many limbs Gibbs had lost. I didn't want to shout right over Gibbs that he's a triple amputee, so instead I hold up three fingers (there's blood all the way up my arm), before grabbing one of the infantry who had come to help and was edging a bit too near to the unsearched area. Last thing we need is another explosion.
I don't remember what else happened. I didn't like war and I didn't want to be there. I wanted it to all go away.
We get him on the stretcher. By now he's had morphine. We're running back through the compound to the patrol base. MERT is on its way. The Afghan family, who had warned us before about there being bombs on the other side of the wall, were disappearing inside as we ran through their home. The dad is there, grabbing his children and herding them inside. Billows of white robes. I'm running alongside with the fluid bag held high. Through the one gap in the wall, someone had spray-painted a yellow circle on the ground, a mark and avoid because we thought another IED was there. Someone yells out for us to jump over it – there's no way around- so we all hop over, careful not to step on it. Five minutes ago, someone had shouted MERT being twelve minutes away.
I'm shouting at Gibbs, but he's not responding anymore and his eyes are dilated.
"WAKE THE FUCK UP! FUCKING WAKE UP!" I slapped him hard on the face, and he responded to that, he snapped out of his delirium and looked in my direction with a shocked and angry expression.

Where's that fucking chopper? As we near the patrol base, people are shouting at the soldiers gathering inside to give them a hand with the stretcher, and suddenly people are crowding around and grabbing the handles off of the others. Someone else grabbed the bag of fluid from me and they took off again in the direction of the HLS, sprinting as fast as they could, with the rest following behind. Where's that fucking chopper?! We get him to the HLS, where the two medics carried on treating him. Suddenly we all heard the Chinook rotors thumping and I looked up and remember seeing MERT screaming around the corner of a hill banking crazily and landing fast. I've never seen a Chinook land like that. They're here. It's all going to be okay now.
The stretcher party had gone on ahead and got him on it. Smudge was there, and suddenly grabbed me and hugged me and that's where I suddenly broke down in sobs, but that ended when someone yelled that we're going to get mortared and take cover. I looked to my left at the field across the valley and saw a plume of white smoke from a field, but my memory ends there, leaving a blank.
Suddenly, it's all over. MERT had gone, racing off into the distance, back to the waiting surgeons at Bastion. We're reorganizing ourselves, still in a state of shock. I'd just vomited, and was spitting out the bile from my mouth. I'm covered in blood. It's everywhere. Little Steve was smoking a fag, hands shaking. He's staring at nothing. My hands are shaking too, my whole body is trembling. I go and wash off the blood, many times over. It's in the grooves of my ring, my watch, fingernails, and ingrained in my skin. I didn't eat anything I touched for a long while afterwards. My voice had also become strained, as if something was restricting my neck. It lasted several days. I had so much blood on my smock and trousers that I threw them on the burns pit and someone gave me theirs. Later on, someone else gave me some new boots and threw my old blood-soaked ones onto the fire.

At FOB Inkerman, we're told Gibbs had died on the way to Bastion. He didn't stand a chance. No one really knew what to say.
Later on, the medical officer and the medic meet up with us and we sit in the sun discussing what had happened. The medic comes up to me and hugs me and starts crying into my shoulder. She was the one who had been sitting next to Gibbs earlier that morning, the one who

had come sprinting in, instructing the other one what to do.
“I hate this. I hate this,” she sobs over and over. She was trying to say something, but was crying too much for me to understand.
“She’s had this kind of thing her whole tour,” the doctor later explained. “She was always on the patrols that got blown up, so she had to deal with all the cat A’s. So, we put her down in Jackson where we thought it would be better for her.”
The drive back to Jackson later was much the same as before. The Sergeant Major still yelled at Vinny, but no one said anything, even when the Mastiff knocked over a telephone pole, or when the Sergeant Major shouted down something about an RPG threat.
Gibbs’s empty seat was opposite me, staring me in the face. The driver had later found an i-pod inside the Mastiff, and when no one claimed it, someone finally worked it out.
“It’s Gibbs’s.”
We later sent it home along with other personal things to his family.
That night, I lay wide awake in my doss bag, staring at the pitch blackness above my head, waiting patiently. Finally, the soft sound of snoring filled the darkness. Silently, I retreated to the depths of the sleeping bag. I curled up into a ball, pressed my face into the crook of my elbow and cried and cried and cried.

After Gibbs was blown up, we waited a day for a replacement team to arrive so we could get back to Bastion for all the follow up stuff that happens, like the repatriation. That was my birthday, and Steve and I had spent most of that day sitting outside the COB. We mainly sat in silence, side by side.
"I can’t stop thinking about it," he eventually murmured.
"Nor can I," I said after a while. He started silently crying again. So did I. Gibbs is gone. The way he was crying and trying to snuggle up to someone. The image in my mind of him lying there as I ran to him. The sound he made when he was trying to breathe.
“I don’t want to do this anymore,” he said.
“Neither do I. I don’t want to go out there again.”
We sat there next to each other for a long time. I looked over at the distant ridge line. A helicopter was silhouetted against the golden sunset, flying back to Bastion. "What the fuck are we doing here, Steve?"
Silence."Dunno mate," he said eventually. Nothing could be worse

than this.
Later on, more of the others joined, and we just sat there. Lee's birthday was the next day, so we opened up some brie cheese, and the rest of the biltong to celebrate our joint birthdays, though it was hard to be happy about anything.
After dark, I had managed to get on a sat phone and called Anna. I sat there in the darkness of the cab in the Teller for a long time, looking at the phone. Eventually I called. Straight away she could tell something was wrong, but I didn't really know how to tell her. Eventually, I just said it. "Gibbs is dead".
I didn't go into details. I just wanted to talk to someone back home. It was hard to know what to say to her. "I really thought we'd all make it".

That evening, I was by the cookhouse, getting a brew. A white pickup truck was parked there with some Chohgees, talking to British officers. One of the Afghan men was there, crying his eyes out and wailing loudly in Pashtun. He was beside himself. In the back of the truck was a dead child, maybe five years old. It looked like she had been shot, because an IED would have done far more damage. The officers seemed very subdued, and were quietly expressing their sympathies to the father via the tangeeman, who carried on sobbing, leaning against the back of the truck. I was quietly watching this all from just within the entrance to the cookhouse.
I hated war. I hated being here. Going out on patrol and walking past people giving you this stare when you smile at them, and not knowing which one of them has just laid an IED to blow you up, or take a shot at you from God knows which compound. I hated getting shot at and not seeing where it was coming from and not being able to do anything but run into cover, not even knowing if there wasn't a bomb there waiting for you. I hated the tension before the shooting begins, listening to the Taliban on the radio commenting on what you are doing, telling each other to get ready, they're coming closer. That was beginning to get to me too. I hated always being on edge about where I stepped. I hated the fact that IEDs were everywhere. I was sick of being scared all the time. I was sick of not being told anything. I hated, and was terrified of going out on the ground. I hated why this kid had died. I didn't know if it was us that shot her

or the Taliban, but it really got to me. She made me think about my nieces, and that really upset me.

Back at the flight line, clambering off the Chinook that got us out of Sangin and brought us back to Bastion, that safe haven in Helmand where soldiers dream about spending their tours. A truck from the CIED lines came and picked us up. The question on everyone's mind was how long we would get to spend at Bastion before we'd have to go out again. Bastion is safe. The rifles get cleaned and handed back into the iso container serving as the armory. Sweaty, heavy dusty body armor gets dumped beside each bed of the tent assigned to each team. Bastion is clean and fresh and sterile. Faded combats get stripped, stuffed into dhobi bags and handed into the Indian guy running the washing machines. He pretends to take care with keeping order, but your white bag is immediately lost among forty other identical white bags. No one cares. You'll find it later. Within three minutes of getting off the truck that brought us from the flight line, I'm naked, fumbling around the tent for some flip flops and a towel and shower gel before hopping over to the row of iso containers fitted out with flushing toilets and showers with a never-ending supply of hot water. Everyone else has found a shower cubicle, and just stand there under the water. Feel the force on the top of your head, close your eyes. Running down your lips, off your chin. The button slowly pops out, the water abruptly stops, so you press it again, turn around and lean back on it to keep it down. Opposite, there's a mirror. Man, I've lost weight. My skin is a lot browner; my hair was a lot longer and matted and greasy. My shoulders are red from the body armor hanging off them and arms are thinner, my chest is smaller, making the clump of identity discs hanging from my neck seem big. On the floor by my feet there's left over bottles of shampoo and conditioners and other lotions which had been sent out to soldiers by loved ones back in the UK. Most important was the nail brush. I picked it up and meticulously began scrubbing my fingers, finger nails, palms, wrists, forearms, elbows and everywhere else that might be hiding ingrained blood.
Later, after an age in the showers, we made our way over to the cookhouse, made up of two enormous cylindrical tents. Fresh food was served. All kinds of meats, vegetables, fruit, puddings. We had

the good fortune of going to dinner just when an American civilian catering company had flown out to Afghan to serve the troops for a few days. They had cooked hundreds of gourmet style meals and were dishing it out to the line of British soldiers. Lobster. Steaks. Shrimp sauce. Mushroom sauce. They had girls with grey t shirts and baseball caps wondering up and down the aisles with more helpings, asking in their American twang if "any 'a y'all want some mo' 'a this here lobster, you just gi' me a holler, ya hear now? Ai be right on o'er."

Later that evening, the OC summoned us to the welfare tent. We gathered on the couches around the TV set, and switched off the ever-present BFBS when he came in, followed by the Sergeant Major. The OC of the Counter IED task force was a well-spoken man, who seemed to have a quiet nature. He listened to each one of us when he asked how the team's morale was doing. He told us we would be here for a few days, to take part in Gibbs's repatriation ceremony.

"I'm keen to get you out on the ground as soon as possible," he said. "It's better that way. I know it's the last thing any of you want to hear, but believe me, you do not want to end your tour like this. The more time you spend here, the harder it will be to go out again. For a few days though, you can relax." He was absolutely right.

Afterwards, by the hospital, the Sergeant Major took us through the drill movements of carrying a coffin onto the aircraft. At the back of the Land Rover was a coffin, weighed down with sandbags. He had to shout to make himself heard each time a helicopter landed on the helipad by the med-centre, blowing out a tsunami of talcum powdery dust. Each time a helicopter landed, a team of RAF firemen ran on board and came out with the stretcher with a man on it. They would quickly place him on a waiting Land Rover converted into an ambulance, which would then rapidly speed off, only to stop right outside the doors of the emergency entrance. There, another team lost no time in taking the stretcher out of the back, only to be lost behind the two swivel doors as they rushed to the operating room. It was all very efficient.

We rehearsed the drill movements taught to us again and again, slowly sweating under the simulated weight of the coffin on our shoulders until we were all confident with the drill.

The parade was later at the airfield, around midnight. Five soldiers had been killed that week, so there were five teams of each man's friends who had just gone through similar ordeals. Five Land Rovers with five coffins sealed shut. One by one, at the Sergeant Major's direction, each team carefully slid their coffin out, raised it onto their shoulders, turned on a heel and began the slow march towards the rear ramp of the waiting C-130. Soldiers on each side facing inwards were called to attention and saluted, as the first of the coffins gradually made its way between them.
We were the last ones. Step by step we followed the bearers ahead of us, trying to step in unison to keep the coffin from bumping. The aircraft's engines were both on and it was very noisy and difficult to hear the commands. On the back of the plane, we joined the others, placing our coffin neatly on the floor. Stood to attention while the padre said whatever prayers padres say over a coffin, making a sign of the cross over each one. Aircrews were already securing each load with straps. Right turn, and march out to a clearing for the bearers.
"HALT! *Aboooouuut*.....TURN!"
"SALUTING! *Saluting to the froooooonnnnt*.....SALUTE!"
We watched, still saluting, as the ramp was raised. Very quickly the engines got louder as they revved and hurled the aircraft down the airstrip and off into the night sky, taking off almost vertically. It disappeared immediately. We'd seen enough aircraft take off and land during the day to know that the pilot would be banking hard left almost immediately to avoid the hills where the Taliban sometimes fired from.

Dawn comes the next morning a few hours later. Inside the tent, with the doors firmly shut, not a single ray of light penetrates the darkness. Everyone is sleeping, deep inside their doss bags. I'd for once had a good night sleep, unafraid because we're in Bastion. Piles of clothes litter the floor around each bed space. In the centre of the room is a table overloaded with *Nuts* magazines, outdated newspapers, and empty boxes of mail which had been handed out the night before. Shredded cardboard from the mail and stale pizza from the late-night Pizza Hut stand by the NAAFI sat on the only chair. On the other side of the tent, in the darkness, someone else has gotten up and was fumbling around with a torch.
At some stage, the team slowly wake up and make their way to the

showers, and then together we head off to the cookhouse. Over breakfast, we discussed what we wanted to do. We had a week at Bastion, largely left to ourselves. So, we decided to go over to the American lines to see what Leatherneck was like.

Leatherneck was adjacent to Bastion, and connected by a regular bus service that drove little over walking speed along flat, straight roads. There were bus stands, and stop signs and military police to make sure all ran smoothly. The buses would always be enveloped by a cloud of brown talcum powdery dust when they stopped to let on passengers.

We spent that week wondering around Bastion and Leatherneck, exploring the American PX, which was far better stocked than the NAAFI. They had a nice coffee outlet which looked similar to a Starbucks or Costa back home. They would usually be crowded by other British tourists who had also just come off the ground for a few days. It was obvious who were the combat troops and who were rear echelon. The soldiers who spent their tour out on the ground wore faded and stained combats from wading through irrigation canals. They had sideburns and long hair and had a petulant attitude to any attempt to try to tidy them up. They stood out from the neater, better presented soldiers who had office and admin jobs. There was an unofficial competition to see if you could survive Bastion without getting your hair cut.

Apart from the repatriation service, the only other thing we had to do was be individually interviewed about what had happened that led to Gibb's death. We were each asked to give details of the terrain, a small map and all our movements. Two soldiers had been killed in the same place in two days, and the army was eager to learn how this had happened.

I answered all the questions my interviewer asked me with detached responses, like a machine.

"It was quiet" I said, half to myself. I was thinking about the flapping cloth in the abandoned courtyard, when Little Steve had remarked how silent it was.

"How do you mean?" she asked.

"I knew something was wrong. Before we even left Jackson, I had a bad feeling." I didn't care how it sounded because it had been bothering me. "Just before the explosion, I had a horrible feeling something was about to happen."

I don't think she knew what to say to that, so we got on with asking the same questions that had been asked hundreds of times after each casualty. When it was over, I walked out of the tent into the bright sunshine, agitated and glad it was finally over.

8
Moshtarak
50 days remaining

Operation Moshtarak was the big offensive of 2010, and involved about 15,000 men. At least I heard it was 15,000 British, American, Canadian and Afghan soldiers who were ear-marked for this offensive, but as usual, none of us knew many details about anything at the time. I found out more from watching Sky News in the NAAFI at Bastion about events that were unfolding right there, than I did by being told. The first time we had officially heard about this big operation was back in December, when Troopie had mentioned that we might be part of a big offensive in the Nadi Ali area, but he called it Operation Monserrat.

It had begun about a week before when we were still in Sangin. All day at the NAAFI and in the squadron TV tent, we watched clips of soldiers being loaded into Chinooks in their long lines, laden down with kit. It was going on just down the road, but so far, we had not been told when it was our turn. It was expected that the enemy would withdraw and rely heavily on IEDs, so there would be a lot of work for the Engineers.

Every day spent at Bastion was a day spent in security. The next day, we were loaded onto a Chinook and flown to yet another small, open aired outpost somewhere in the Nadi Ali region.

We're on another task. It's a road running along a canal and it's filled with accumulated scrap metal. It's taken two days to cover just two hundred metres because literally every single step produces a metal tone which has to be dug up with a bayonet, only to find a rusted nut or bolt which is then flung into a canal. On our left is the wide canal about twenty metres across. On our right flank is an open field bordered by a treeline.

There's been no sign of the enemy for some days now, only the occasional distant explosion. Usually that meant someone had just stepped on an IED. Hopefully it was the enemy scoring an own goal and not any civilians, but there was no way of telling. We always

knew if it were ours. Our casualties would always summon a helicopter to the area of the explosion.
One explosion in particular happened much closer, beyond the trees. That explosion was different from the others, it was a strange mixture of the normal *Boom!* with a *Peeeeooooouuu!* We later learnt it was an EFP. Explosively Formed Projectile. The projectile can be anything really, and it shoots across from the side like a sideways explosion of fire and earth and molten metal.
We all stopped. There was the usual silence of maybe a second, and then screaming. Lots of shouting in a foreign, European sounding language. We stood facing the tree line at the other end of the field, unable to run over and help. It had taken a whole day to search the same distance. No one could see anything. No one said anything for a long time. The screaming was horrible, it went on and on and was only drowned out by the sound of the American casevac chopper, The Pedro.
"Danish," someone said at last.
We learnt later that when one of the Danish vehicles were blown up, in the confusion a Humvee driven by two Afghan soldiers also drove over into the canal, drowning them both.

Later that day Little Steve found an improvised claymore along the raised road we were working on. He was slowly approaching a small mound of earth like an ant hill, and long before he neared it, he was suspicious. A classic marker. He signals us to halt, we take a knee and cover him while he breaks off the road and slowly circles around the mound of earth until he is twenty metres behind it, facing back at us. He raises his rifle to inspect the ant hill through the SUSAT and before long he spots a wire on the reverse side of the mound to where we were coming from. The ATO went forward to dismantle the device, emptying the home-made explosive into the canal where it floated down river like an oil spill. He showed us the shrapnel that made up the claymore. Scrap metal. Explosively Formed Projectile. Had Steve not listened to his instinct, had the ECM not worked, or had we not bothered with those exhausting, annoying isolations, all four of us would have been blown to shreds into the water.

It wasn't long after finding the claymore. I'm on the left of the road, sweeping the side of the wheel rut and down the bank leading to the

water's edge. Steve is doing the same on his side while Lee and Big Steve are following behind. For reasons we never really knew, we still had not received a battle casualty replacement for Gibbs, but it might have been that by then they had all gone to other teams.
All the metal in the road is making our progress unbelievably slow. Each piece of metal has to be dug up and thrown into the river before the ground can be checked again. It's incredibly tedious. A sudden storm appears out of nowhere and it pours with heavy torrential rain. Before long, everything has turned into slippery mud. Water cascades down the front of my helmet, I can feel my underwear getting wet, making me angry. Then just as suddenly, the rain stops. Down by the bank of the canal, something catches my eye. It's a footprint, right by the water. It's facing away from the water, up the slope towards the road I am standing on. It's also alone. Whoever had made the footprint had no reason to be down there. It was not a crossing point, there was nothing special about the location. They also must have come by boat, stepping off onto the river bank, but had not walked up to the road. I tell the others to halt while I make my way down the slope towards the footprint. As I do so, my Vallon gets a hit on metal. I crouch down and carefully sweep the ground with two fingers in a sideways motion, beginning at my feet. A few inches away, the soil becomes soft as I find the filled in hole. Slowly, carefully I begin digging, scooping out handfuls of reddish-brown earth. I'm lying prone, and so are the others. It's not long before I uncover a white surface. Immediately I stop and yell "Find!" The ATO comes and takes over while I wait up on the road with the others. He comes back, telling his team to send a ten-liner. What I had found was a cache. All the components to make up four victim-operated IEDs. The enemy must have used small boats to travel up and down the canal rather than using the road at night, which they knew was mined.

We spent three days clearing that road by the canal, with the tall trees in the distant getting nearer at the end of each day. We had a sniffer dog and his handler with us, and sometimes we would send the dog to investigate suspicious patches of ground. When the dog sniffed plastic, explosives or anything else that shouldn't be in the ground, it would turn and look at us, with one leg cocked in the air. Then one of us would go and investigate while all the others would

discreetly take cover, trying not to be rude.
We didn't know why we were clearing the road. It seemed to go off into nowhere, too far away to be seen by the nearest check point. We slept there every night under the stars, quietly complaining that no one would be able to monitor our progress. When this was pointed out the next day, we had a small area cleared at the end of the day to leave a two-man team to watch the road. They were snipers and did a good job at concealing themselves in their position.
We were returning back to the CP after our third day. Three days of patrolling out to where we had searched up to the previous day, slowly clearing the road, and collapsing back to the CP before dusk. Being the road that led out of the CP, we were forced to use the same route repeatedly. Fortunately, it had been quiet for those three days, apart from the Danish getting blown up. We had finally reached the end of the road where the tall trees were and heading back to the CP. I was walking just behind the quad and trailer, which carried all our heavy kit for us. Off to our right, across the canal I see a man on a red motor bike suddenly rev his engine and speed away. As he did so, just as I begin to react to what I am seeing, the earth on that side of the canal explodes in a heavy detonation. I either dove or fell onto the ground, and saw Lee dive down as well. The thunderclap echoes across the fields in all directions. The whole multiple is on the ground, waiting for events to unfold. Someone was shouting "IDF! IDF!" Mortars.
"Is anyone hit?" someone else called. Everyone called out our names from where we were laying. No casualties. We wait for more impacts, spread out along the road, lying flat and looking at each other. The huge cloud of dust had blown our way, smelling of cordite, but as the minutes ticked by, we realised we were not getting mortared. It had been an IED, on the other side of the canal. The enemy, who had been watching us do the same thing each day had buried one of their improvised claymores on the bank opposite us. They had hoped that the shrapnel would blow out across to our side and detonated when the quad I was walking behind was in line with it. Luckily, all the shrapnel either went up, or missed us all.
Three days of boredom and then sudden violence. We had been lucky with our push into enemy territory. The Danish troops on our flank hadn't been.

Those Moshtarak days are now all a faded memory. We were loaded onto choppers and flown around the area to either clear a device someone had found, or search a road that led into enemy territory. Details of the offensive were not known to us. We showed up at a task with our kit and went about our business, either blowing up the device in situ or dismantling it. All that mattered was the number of days remaining.

Nights were always behind walled compounds, dossing down wherever there was space on the ground. One night we found ourselves in a compound full of French soldiers and I remember listening in on their conversations but understanding only bits and pieces.

We had been in one compound for a couple of days and had sallied out to deal with just one IED. The rest of the time had been spent all day doing nothing but play cards and wait for scoff.

The Scouse came up with a plan. He had found out that the Squadron had no immediate need of us for a few days, when we were scheduled to another PB to help them with a push down a road. In the meantime, we were treading water in the middle of nowhere.

"We're going back to Bastion," he told us one evening. "Next supply chopper that comes, we're on it. If we're waiting for a task, then we'll wait back at Bastion. Those bastards will just keep us out here for no reason."

All other teams seemed to be getting preferential treatment. Our team came from another regiment as an attachment. Throughout our tour we had noticed this and came the logical conclusion: we were EOD's Ginger Step-Children.

So that's what we did. The next day, a Sea King arrived and unloaded its payload of supplies. As we loaded it up with the outpost's rubbish, we had our kit on hand. We climbed aboard, sitting on either side, with a chest high mountain of rubbish between us.

The Scouse must have gotten into trouble when we got back to CIED lines. He might have been frosty at times since he took over as team leader, but commandeering a chopper so that we could have a few days back at Bastion showed us a what kind of leader he was.

23/2/10 Bastion. *Received warning order tonight. We're going to Nad-i-Ali tomorrow. Its amazing how your heart drops when you get news like that. 44 days remaining.*

The helicopter dropped us off in the middle of a green field the day after I wrote that journal entry. As usual, the infantry cordon was dotted around the makeshift perimeter, keeping an eye out as we piled clumsily out of the Sea King and huddled together for protection from the powerful downdraft as the chopper took off again. In another couple of seconds, it was gone, racing off at low level to another destination.

Check Point Bennett used to be someone's home. An Afghan family had once lived there for generations, unaware that their neighbourhood was being discussed by Moshtarak planners in Whitehall, and maps of their fields and homes were being studied in detail. In any case, those were days when we were still anxious about our two-week leave period, and none of us knew or cared about anything else apart from going home.
I never did find out if the family had been forced out by us or the Taliban before their compound was turned into a military outpost, but there definitely had been fighting there because the walls were pock marked with bullet holes of different shapes and sizes. Much later on when we had some more time on our hands, I took a photo of Little Steve sitting in front of this bullet riddled wall, cleaning his weapon. He's got his t-shirt off, and catching a tan with a pull-through in the barrel. At the time I took it, I thought, what a cool photo.
I never thought about the people who once lived there, or where they had spent the winter.

The infantry unit garrisoned there were equipped with Jackals – open topped vehicles resembling rally cars armed with heavy machine guns. One of the Jackals was parked in a gap in the wall, acting as the back gate. The sentry on stag sat in the gunner's seat with his body armour and helmet on, behind a grenade machine gun, keeping a lookout. Behind him, behind the walls of the compound, soldiers slept wherever they could. Most had erected ponchos against the walls and slept on inflatable roll mats which kept losing air

throughout the night so that by dawn you would feel stones digging into all the painful joints of your body.
There was only one building in the compound, with three rooms. One of those rooms was used as the ops room. The other two were packed with stores of food and water. There was room for a few soldiers to claim a space for them to sleep in under a roof as long as they slept against the walls. Fortunately, those sleeping outside under the stars, the Afghan winter had quickly disappeared.

24/2/10 *They flew us into Nadi Ali AO this afternoon. We're in a small compound with the Royal Welsh, its back to basics again. The front gate is a Jackal. In fact, all the sangers are jackals driven into position so their guns can bear.*
FLET is a couple of kilometres down the road. Estimates 80-100 Taliban. There's a couple of areas of interest they want us to check out tomorrow which they don't want to go into because they think its booby trapped. So we have to check it out for them. 43 days remaining.

After the O Group that evening, the Scouse came back with more details of the situation we had landed ourselves into. The road running past Check Point Bennett ran in one long straight line as far as the eye could see. It eventually led to another equally isolated patrol base, called PB Schoolhouse. We dominated our end of this road, and the Taliban dominated their end, two kilometres away.
The Brigade Recce Force had first gone down the road to try find out a bit about the enemy in the area. They had no incidents involving IEDs, and it must have been pretty easy going mainly because this was an area ISAF hadn't ever gone down before. The entire area used to be all Taliban controlled before Op Moshtarak was launched. That single excursion by the BRF had however immediately gripped the attention of the Taliban, and suddenly IEDs began being reported by locals. The day before we arrived, an American counter IED team had been blown up in one of their armoured vehicles when they were trying to officially clear the route.
The Americans were equipped with a series of enormous heavily armoured vehicles which were supposed to find bombs in a variety of ways. They each have a different role to play and are all slowly driven down a road in single file. The lead vehicle has big heavy

rollers in front of it, designed to roll over an IED and blow it up first before the vehicle itself drives over it. The entire armoured train had lumbered painstakingly slowly in the sweaty heat when suddenly one of these rollers triggered off a pressure plate. The explosion must have been enormous, because it blew the heavy-duty wheels, together with its metal bracing a hundred metres in all directions, disabling the lead vehicle. Fortunately, the V-shaped design of these vehicles worked. The wheels deliberately sheared off, keeping the force of the blast away from the main body, saving the three Americans inside.

It was then that they made their mistake. The commander of the team ordered the recovery vehicle forward. The poor driver was forced to overtake the whole column in order to reach the lead vehicle. This meant driving out into unsearched ground, something which made all of us listening to this story groan at hearing, wondering why the Americans would do such a thing. Although his vehicle had a V-shaped hull and wheels designed to sheer off in an explosion, it did not have rollers out in front. When the wheels hit the second IED in his path, it was directly under the driver. He didn't stand a chance.

The infantry company tasked with clearing and keeping this road open was commanded by a Major, a worried looking man who seemed to do his best in achieving his objectives given to him each night when he spoke to his superiors at Bastion on the secure-line. Now he had been sent a Search Team to replace the Americans, who had become understandably unenthusiastic about returning to the scene where they had lost a friend so recently. None of us would have liked to have gone back to the compound where Gibbs had been blown up. Whenever possible, the army tried to move teams around after a casualty. They didn't want revenge influencing people's behaviour.

Now we knew there were definitely IEDs on the road, no one wanted to go out on the ground. It had only been a week since one of our team members had been killed, and no one wanted do any searching ever again. The psychological impact of seeing one of your friends being blown up is enormous. With such horrific memories engraved forever in your mind, the fear of walking on ground, never knowing if each step could be your last can be overpowering.

That night the mortar teams had a fire mission, and had kept everyone up. Smudge was lying on his roll mat across the room from me, doing a cross word puzzle by the light of his head torch, watching me jerk each time a mortar fired. One would fire with a short loud *bang!* making me jump in my doss bag. Then a few seconds later another would fire, making me jump again. I couldn't help it.
"I can't stop jumping!" I eventually yelled in exasperation.
"I know," he said sympathetically. "I know."

The next morning, greying light. Afghan soldiers standing along the wall, joking with each other in Pashtun. Others adjusting their straps the way they had been taught in their basic training. Some of our soldiers are drinking last minute cups of ration-coffee, waiting to get a move on.
The patrol set out in staggered formation from the walls of the compound. There were a lot of us. Everyone cocks their weapon as they leave the gate, and dresses to either side of the road, leaving a ten-metre gap between each man. ANA are mixed in among us, and we also have a couple of Jackals driving slowly along, bristling with machine guns.
The Search Team is acting as Quick Reaction Force, only searching any really dodgy bits of road. The rest of the road, as long as it was low threat, was to be done by the barma team.
As the morning progressed, more and more locals came out and went about their day as if forty soldiers armed to the teeth walking slowly past was a normal occurrence, which it was. The main road was dotted with the local one-room side shops with old men sitting in clusters outside the entrance, and children flocking to the side of the road. Eventually one of them would be nominated by the others to voice their interest in us, bravely calling out "Biscuit! Biscuit!"
Moshtarak was a never-ending series of searches and helicopter rides, the snap crackle pop of the opening burst of gunfire, and that whistling noise that rounds sometimes make when they fly overhead. But that first search I remember in particular because suddenly, that noise Gibbs was making as he was trying to breathe came into my head. I kept scanning the walls and hedges around us as we patrolled along the road, tried to watch what I was doing, trying to ignore it. I couldn't shake it.

We're on another isolation, searching for any possible wires leading up to the road from which the bomb could be detonated. The road we've been on has had problems with snipers taking pot shots at the patrol as we try to search it. Each time there's some shooting, everyone drops down where they are and waits until its safe again, assuming the escorting infantry have taken care of the problem. Our isolations are taking about an hour to cover about a fifty-metre stretch of road. Half an hour walking slowly off to the side, into the fields, walking parallel to the road. Crossing over the road to the other side and then half an hour back to the convoy. Each time walking in single file, following the lead searcher, the only searcher as he picks out a path for us to follow. Everyone slowly creeping behind him either carrying ECM, keeping a look out, or both. And the crucial man with the command wire detector, raking the ground behind him. Each time the man in front stops to alter direction to keep an unpredictable path, the rest of us drop to one knee and watch the rooftops.

We've just left the cover of a wall, moving down the side of this field. At that time of year, the crops sown the previous winter had sprouted and were now waist high, and very green. Across the field were more walls forming a corner, and an alleyway.

Even now, I can still see him. He was clad in black, and was loitering in the alleyway as if waiting for his friends. Twice I glance at him, unable to make up my mind if he is a threat or not. The infantry are protecting us. Surely, they must have checked him out by now. Still, he makes me nervous, and too late I realise why: all the children have gone.

I call a halt and tell the others, and raise my rifle to him to see him through my SUSAT, just in time to see his raised rifle. It looked like it was pointing straight at me. My finger moves to the safety above the trigger, but he fired first. The percussions of each round being heard through the SUSAT vision.

Suddenly I am on the ground. There's more gunfire, that distinctive noise of AK47s, mixed with cracking and whistling. The infantry fire from their cordon, inwards into the alleyway. We're all still on the ground. I'm lying on my back with my legs buckled under me. I knew I had not been hit but I still patted myself down and looked at my fingers for blood. I was shocked at how close and sudden that had been. Everything had happened in a few seconds. Smudge is the man in front of me, and in a brief lull, he says in a low voice, 'Go! Go!' pointing to the wall we left. It's only a few metres away and one by one we sprint back bent over double. No one is hit. The man in the alleyway is gone, though whether the infantry killed him or not no one could say.

I was angry with myself that he had been faster than me. I wanted to rewind the clock again, so I could be faster than him.

Nights would be spent in the nearest compound. Never out in the open. Sometimes the home had already been taken over by the army and turned into a little fortress. And sometimes the family was still there, at least until we told them their home with its valuable walls was needed to secure the area. It would always be officers negotiating with the family through an interpreter, persuading them to take the chit where they could show at the gates of some army base where everything would be better again. Asking them if there were any friends or family nearby where they could stay that night. There was never any chance for those people to say no. Their home was going to be occupied no matter how much they protested and how little warning we gave, watching as Jackals filled with food water and ammunition were offloaded into their immaculate houses. Choosing a home depended on how far down the road we had advanced that day. When we reached a particular point, we would lay up for the night in the nearest walled property. Compound crashing, we called it.

It was obvious the Afghans kept their homes well. One woman I remembered crying and shouting at the tangeeman, which was unusual in such a male dominated culture. After the terms were given, the officer in charge was satisfied that the family had accepted the offer and were packing their belongings. The tangeeman later told me that the woman had told him that she would rather die than leave her home.

That bit got lost in translation.

Sleeping behind thick high walls gives you a great feeling of security, even if you are only a small group of men trying to push into enemy territory. Of course, when you get woken up for your turn on stag, get out of your doss bag, get your boots on, helmet on, body armour on, grab your rifle, climb the ladder, creep low across the rooftop to the machine gun, tap the other guy on the shoulder, when he leaves you alone, you're not as secure anymore. It's monotonous, and scary. The lives of everyone sleeping down in the compound depend on you. One Afghan National Army compound had been relieved by one of our units only to discover that all of them had either been shot in their sleep or had had their throats slit. I stare at a shadow for a long time until I cannot hold my breath anymore and exhale as softly as I can. I'm certain someone is there, crouching in an over watch position, his AK trained between my eyes while others are filing past to take up their positions to overrun the compound and cut the heads of everyone inside with those sadistically small knives. Very slowly I have been reaching for the NVG monocle, finally raise it to my face and turn it on. Machine gun stock in my shoulder, finger on trigger. The world erupts into alien green. There's no one there.

The next day was spent behind the walls. There must have been twenty or thirty men lying in the sun, with the lucky ones able to sleep in the shade. We powdered our feet, planned what rations we would eat for lunch and cleaned weapons.
We had been in the field for a few weeks now and no one had fresh clothes anymore. Prickly heat was back, but this time there was no med centre to go to. The medic gave out ointment, but this didn't solve the problem. Individual wet wipe supplies were carefully monitored. A few soldiers had brought bottles of shampoo with them, and this was shared out as improvised washing powder. Just outside the walls was a small knee-high irrigation canal water which we used to fill a bucket with and were able to do some handwashing. I rinse off my underwear and U backs and watch the water quickly become black, even without shampoo. I rinsed my clothes twice before using shampoo, and still poured away brown black water. Of course, being outside the walls was risky and there was only one place you could safely squat without being seen by snipers.
The toilet were two more buckets we had commandeered, and was just round the corner from the main courtyard. When one was free, I grabbed a wag-bag (both wag bags and wet wipes were equally as important as ammunition), lined it around the mouth of the bucket, trousers by ankles and squatted in the stress position next to The Scouse. We both looked at each other and burst out laughing, but my

thighs were quickly burning, being held in position at right angles. How much time you spent on the toilet depended entirely on how strong your leg muscles were.

Lee was on stag when the sniper began taking his first shots at us. They were loud cracks flying over the compound walls. There were only two stag points, and both were getting shot at each time they showed their head. Lee eventually had to roll off the rooftop with a loud "fuuuuuuck!"
The whole afternoon was spent trying to work out where the sniper was, with our sniper studying satellite maps and the terrain. We were safe behind the thick walls, but no one was allowed out. Later on, I managed to make a call to Anna.
"So where are you now?" I asked with the usual meaningless chit chat.
"I'm just shopping in Tescos" she said.
I paused at that. "You're in Tesco?" Another pause. "That is so weird."
I never wanted to share details of what was happening, and so letters and phone calls became repetitive and boring. I didn't tell her about snipers or the claymores or listening to the Danish the other week. Yesterday we had all had a huge scare. There had been an IED discovered just outside the entrance on the main road. Little Steve had found it buried on the edge of a huge puddle in the road. It was exactly where you would walk as you skirted around the water. Later when the ATO went to take care of it we stayed back in the compound, our search stalled just after we had begun. We were all in the courtyard, lying in the sun when without warning, a booming explosion. A tsunami of dust travels across the mud walls and earthen floor, while a few seconds later, branches rain down on us from the sky. I remember Smudge and I looking at each other in a split second of shock and inaction. There's that awful silence again just after an explosion. I remember my thoughts: NOOO! Not again! No! Fuck! No! No! No!
Now I am running with a Vallon in my hand. It's turned on and making the start-up beeps while it calibrates. I know there's a tourniquet in my map pocket. The only other thing I remember is being stopped at the doorway by another soldier. I had been running

out with a Vallon but no helmet or body armour.
"Don't worry lads," he's saying. "Controlled detonation."

We've been finding The Scouse a bit prickly lately. He had replaced Troopie, who had gone on to be the RESA for one of the Gurkha teams when their ATO was killed. He had joined the team as an outsider and we were a bit cautious of him. He could be short tempered. Usually, the four searchers would just glance at each other, saying nothing.

That day there was some fighting up ahead of our search. The dried grass on my side of the road had all been burnt, leaving bunches of hard, blackened stalks. Every time there was some gunfire crackling overhead, the whole search team would flinch as one, into a half crouch, before cautiously resuming our search. The enemy a few compounds away were trying to stop our progress, and our infantry were holding them off. Everything centred on the slow, methodical progress of the four searchers who were trying to ignore the fighting around them and focus their attention on the ground.

A sudden burst of gunfire and loud snapping sent us all flat on the ground. My Vallon was lying next to me, giving a continuous *beeeeep* that it makes when it is dropped, and I was lying on my back, trying to reach over to restart it when the man behind me grabbed my boot. He had crawled forward to me, following the path I had cleared.

"Mate, are you hit?" he asks breathlessly.

No one had gotten up yet. I look down at him. "I'm okay."

"Fuck me, you went down fast. I thought you'd been shot!"

When diving down, searchers have to learn to spin around and dive down behind them. It's no use throwing yourself on the ground in front of you because that has not been searched. The only safe ground is behind, so that's where you aim for. To the soldier looking after me as I searched, it looked like I had been hit.

We picked ourselves up again and started where we had left off, taking two steps backwards for the overlap before searching forwards again. It wasn't long before I came across a hole in the ground, about as big as a large cooking pot.

"Check on."

In training, everyone is taught to lie down prone each time one of us investigates something. In reality, everyone just drops to one knee

and waits. It's too exhausting to get up and down every minute or so. We only got down when one of us thought he was on to something. This time, I turned around and motioned for everyone to get down before I continued.
The hole I found was baffling. It looked like a canon strike from a helicopter. We had had some sporadic air cover, but the Apache was always called away after a few minutes to help other call signs. To one side of the hole was a small groove in the mud, leading to another smaller hole, just big enough to put a battery pack into it. Both holes were empty.
I had been carefully excavating both sites for a few minutes when I hear The Scouse calling out from road.
"This isn't Time Team! Is it an IED or not?"
I ignored him, carried on carefully clearing away soil. The golden rule in Search is to never rush a searcher. The Scouse had come up behind me, peering over at the hole I was investigating and began berating me for taking so long over something that was obviously an Apache strike. I continued, taking as long as I needed and deliberately stepped into the hole. Little Steve and Lee had listened to the exchange from where they lay on the road, biding their time. Neither were happy with what they had heard.
After lunch, I knew I had to say something. He was a staff sergeant and I was only a sapper, and to confront someone who is four ranks higher than you, telling them they are wrong, is asking for trouble. But I couldn't leave it. I debated it in my mind a few minutes before thinking: Screw it man, I'll probably be dead by the end of this week.
I went over to where The Scouse sat, squatting in front of him, leaning forward on my rifle for balance. I told him that he needed to trust us and let us do our job, but above all, never rush a searcher. He kept telling me he could see what it was and that I was taking too long. Both of us were irritable with each other. He was a staff sergeant; I was a sapper. But I was a searcher, and at the end of the day it was me who would pay for it.
"You're not going to die if you're wrong," I said. "I am."
We were both aware that the infantry major was sitting a few metres away and was obviously listening, but he didn't say anything.
The two holes I had found were a worrying sign. Someone had used the canon strike as an already dug hole, and buried the battery off to

the side in the smaller hole. Later they had decided to use the explosives somewhere else and dug it up again. It meant they were ignoring the road and targeting the searchers off to the sides, myself and Little Steve.

I am just behind the Jackal, getting pretty bored. It was a hot day, loads of flies. I had taken a bunch of photos mainly to pass the time, while occasionally getting up and moving on a few steps with the rest of the patrol as the road ahead was slowly cleared, only to take yet another defensive position facing outwards. The infantry barma team were searching low threat areas, giving us a break until we came to the high risk.

I had just put my camera away when the air explodes around us. *SNAP POP, CRACK*! a bunch of whistling over us, among us. From the left. The barma team diving in all directions. One guy for a moment had both his feet sticking in the air as he flew to the ground. I was already hard up against the Jackal, flattening myself against it. I don't even remember diving. Everyone is crawling. The air above me is making strange sounds, loud and frightening.

CRACK, POP.

Really loud snapping sounds, and whistles. It's like someone snapping a belt right in your ear. I was terrified. The Jackal had begun firing back almost immediately with the machinegun mounted in the passenger seat. Being trapped in the seat, the man had no choice but swing the gimpy around and start spraying everything.

I crawl forward. Everyone lying flat and crawling to the other side of the road towards where the shooting was coming from. One of the Welsh Guards was there. He screamed out "there!" and began rapidly letting off rounds. I ran to him, shooting at the same area he was shooting at. The machine gun right behind me was blasting away. Soldiers on either side of me shooting.

The fear. There wasn't really any cover because of the long grass we were shooting through. If you lay prone you wouldn't see anything, so you just stand there, half crouching. I fired and fired and fired and fired at everything in front of me, and the Taliban did the same back at us, both sides shooting through the long grass that divided us.

Stoppage.

I'm in a half crouch, fingers trembling as I went through the stoppage drills. Cocking handle to the rear. Cleared chamber.

Breathe. Calm down calm down calm down calm down. Magazine out, new one in. Working parts forward. SUSAT pointing at some bushes where I think there's some movement and I let loose at that. There was popping and whizzing noises all over the place. Something cracks in my ear and I flinch and let out a "fuck sake!" and drop down.

One of the Welsh Guards just above me on the heavy machine gun is firing. Its deafening.

Three Taliban had been seen by a big tree and were hugging the ground around it. They were pretty close. The closest I'd seen the enemy. The Scouse fired a UGL - I was right behind him and saw the grenade go high into the air and land right among them and exploded. Someone was yelling "bulls' eye! bulls' eye!"

All of a sudden, I saw one of the Taliban clearly. He was on his knees and seemed stunned. It looked like he didn't know where he was. About ten of us fired into him. For a moment he was there in my SUSAT, then his body suddenly tensed up and he fell forward. His face stayed the same, with his mouth open. It looked like he had been screaming.

The Major was getting a grip of the situation. "From now on, only gimpys and UGLs fire," he was shouting in both directions.

But everything was suddenly quiet. We were doing a head count, making sure none of our guys were hit.

During the lull, myself and Big Steve were detailed to collect all the Vallons that had been scattered everywhere on the road when the barma team had bomb-bursted into cover. All the Vallons had been making the high pitch *beeeeeeeep* during the entire contact, from when they had been dropped. We cleared a section of the road and marked it off as having been searched for the infantry to have some safe ground in case we were attacked again. Off to the right, the ANA were coming in.

I didn't know it at the time but they had been trying to flank the Taliban position further along the road. Apparently during the mad shooting-frenzy, one of the ANA with us on the road had fired his RPG at what he thought was the enemy, but turned out to be Afghan soldiers. One of them was brought in with a horrific foot wound. Most of the inside of his foot had gone, with the end of his boot still attached by a thin strip. He was being propped up between two others, with his head slumped forward and dangling between his

shoulders. Another soldier seemed alright but had taken little bits of frag all over his body. The man with the foot wound was helped into the quad trailer, where the medic went to work. The other soldier was getting in it but first had to show his wounds, with the tangeeman explaining what had happened, before being allowed to get evacuated. They were both driven back down the road to the CP.
A few of the Welsh Guards wanted to assault the known position where we thought one of the Taliban had fled into, which turned out to be a mosque.
"We could cut right across this field in a section attack," the man next to me was saying. We were still in our firing positions facing outwards, keeping our weapons covering the area where the enemy had been killed. Nothing was moving. I just crouched there with the others, listening to the corporal striding towards the sergeant in charge of the platoon, dragging one of the younger soldiers behind him by his body armour.
"Jacko's not fired a single fookin' round!" he was shouting, leaving a sheepish looking private with the sergeant to explain himself.
We set fire to the tall grass that both sides had been shooting through, but the Taliban left us alone after that.
It was only that evening as I lay in my doss bag, staring up at the stars that I began to realise just how fortunate everyone had been. Those Taliban who had ambushed must have been waiting in that mosque long before any of our infantry cordon had arrived that morning. They must have watched them getting into place, deliberately leaving them alone, instead waiting for us to finally reach the stretch of road that was their killing ground. When they all opened up at such close range, every single round had passed through without hitting anyone.
The nightmare that night was of the man in my sights jerking violently forward as his stomach took a burst of rounds. His screaming.
I woke up sometime before dawn and found that I had been crying in my sleep.

A lone figure stood in the road in the distance, and another shorter figure joined him. Little Steve spotted him and had halted the search. He and I were crouching where we had stopped searching and scoping them out through our SUSATs. The man left the boy and

walked back into the tall yellow grass that bordered the road each side. He hadn't a care in the world. We didn't know we had been looking at the enemy until he left the boy in the road to watch us. Then he was gone. We all know something is up over there, but there's nothing for it but to continue with our slow progress.
Towards late afternoon, we approach the same spot we had seen earlier. It's been quiet all day, but we had seen some families leaving their homes carrying their belongings.
The tangeeman, always loitering close to the commander of the patrol, stands with a walkie talkie in front of him listening for enemy chatter. Whenever he hears anything, he interprets it and that gets relayed to us at the front.
"Taliban says 'get ready.'"
We all stop. Another ambush up ahead. The boy is gone, leaving no one in sight in all directions, an obvious combat indicator. Behind us, the Grown Ups are discussing a course of action. Little Steve, Lee and I all squatted where we had searched up to, disinterested and enjoying the pause in the search. As long as I didn't have to put one foot in front of the other, I didn't care who was going to ambush us. Smudge called us back in, so we marked the limits of our lanes and walked back while a Jackal made its way forward.
"That's it for the day lads," said Smudge. "Fuck 'em, let 'em wait".
We bedded down for the night in the adjacent compound. In the morning we awoke to find the Taliban had flooded the road. They had diverted the water from the canals either side onto the road, creating huge puddles that turned out to be knee deep in some places.
But we were waiting for the Americans. They were supposed to come back to help us clear through this damn road, and they arrived in style. They had huge armoured vehicles with a variety of devices to detect IEDs in the road.
Two US soldiers clambered down the ladder to one of their vehicles. They all had USMC labelled on their combats. One of them began scanning the ground around him and said loudly to the other:
"I don't see any civilians, Cpl M___. What does that tell us?"
It was obvious he wanted everyone to listen.
"It tells us that the enemy must be close by," said his colleague in an equally loud voice. It was almost a performance, with the actors speaking more to the audience than to each other.

The four of us, squatting together on the road, just watched these strangers as they tried to subtly teach us about combat indicators. The commanders were all discussing how we would share the work. The Americans were trained to clear roads from their vehicles, while we did it on foot. We thought they were lucky to have such a well-equipped army, while they thought we were just crazy. At least they didn't have to worry about snipers or ambushes as well as bombs. Maybe we were crazy. Who the hell would do this kind of job?
The commanders are talking a lot, looking at the flooded road. The American commander was shaking his head. He said it was not possible. He had a point, none of our search equipment would work through water whether it was vehicle mounted or carried on foot. Before long, they mounted their vehicles and began the slow trek back to their base.
That night, a chopper delivered a water pump with two RAF firemen to set up the hoses. Another Chinook delivered a digger and a plant op from the Royal Engineers. The next day we loaded the water pump onto the bucket of a digger and drove to the edge of the first puddle. It took over an hour to pump out the water, and then we searched through the muddy slush up to the small dry island created by a high point in the road.
We did this for three days.

25 days remaining. I am called up by Smudge. A local shopkeeper has tipped us off about an IED just outside his home. He wanted it removed because of his children, but worst of all, it's on my side of the road. My heart sinks to the bottom of my stomach when I hear this task, but I just look back at him through my blast proof sunglasses.
I don my body armour, weapon and helmet and leave the safety of the compound we had all stopped for lunch in.
It's not a maybe, not even a very likely. There is definitely an IED there, and I'm finally trapped. I'd seen it happen to Gibbs, and now it will happen to me. I was the worst searcher in training, and Gibbs had been the best. Training didn't guarantee anything. Luck was all that mattered.
Smudge leads me a few metres up the road to the Jackal that would provide cover if anyone took a shot at me. It would also provide cover to others from any explosions. He points to a large tree about

twenty metres away.
"He says it's between us and that tree."
I'm turning on my Vallon, pretending to be interested in adjusting it to the correct setting.
Beep Beep Beep Beep.
He puts his hand on my shoulder. "Take your time," he says quietly.
I don't say anything. He's got the med-kit there with him, and I know he'll run to me without thinking the way I had run to Gibbs without thinking. I remembered that journalist I spoke to on the plane. Everyone on this bloody road will live except me.
I prayed to God. I prayed a lot, for God to rescue me and show me where it was. Ahead of me, the ground looked as innocent and benign as it always does. I stand there for a minute, creeping my eyes on every single inch of ground I have to cover to get to the tree, even using my rifle scope to zoom in.
Nothing stands out. I begin the long, slow sweeps of the Vallon and take a step forward. The ground doesn't explode, so I take another step. It might have taken fifteen minutes to traverse just a few metres, the distance a toddler might throw a ball. I checked absolutely everything.
Then an odd thing happens.
My eyes become drawn to a particular patch of ground, where the grass begins. It's an exact spot, like a pinpoint. It's still far away, and so I divert my attention to the ground right in front of me. But my eyes go back to this spot again, and at the same time I knew with absolute certainty that's where it was.
"It's there," I quietly said out loud to myself. However much I looked down at my feet, my eyes would make a beeline, as if distracted, back to the same patch of ground. It was a very strange experience, to not be in complete control of your body.
When I finally reached the grass, my Vallon gave the dual-tone. For some time, I had been nearing this small patch of ground, about as big as a coin, now more curious than scared.
I put the Vallon down behind me, lay down prone before it and carefully brushed the top soil with sideway motions back towards me. When I got to a tiny speck of white plastic, I stopped.
When the ATO detonated this IED, I didn't bother to watch it. Smudge and I sat side by side against the Jackal, feeling the shockwave travel through our bodies.

“I feel sick,” he said.

It was a long time before I spoke about any of my experiences in Afghanistan. But it was longer still before I told anyone about how my eyes kept looking away from the ground at my feet and gravitated to where the booby trap lay. Whenever I did mention it, people would pass it off as intuition or something like that. Then I would say, no you don’t understand. And I would try and tell them again: I wasn’t guessing. I knew where it was. It was like knowing the contents of a book without having read it. My eyes kept going to the exact spot, the way the steering of your car is in need of realigning and keeps veering left and you have to compensate. It was one of the strangest experiences of my life, when I cried out to God and within minutes, I knew the exact location.

We’re in another compound, another home. The owner had contacted ISAF to have a claymore taken care of because his children played nearby. We had trekked in the fields in thick mud, making faster time than had we stuck to the road. The home we were going to was further into Taliban territory, but we were not staying there. Only going there, taking care of business and then getting out again. It was partly to show the enemy that we could do that kind of thing if we wanted to. We didn’t have to stick to the road.
The courtyard had four or five young kids playing in it, with an old man. He was speaking to the tangeeman, who went on to explain to us his request. We needed to throw him out of the compound, so that the Taliban, who were always watching, would see that we were there uninvited. He didn’t want them coming back to him after we had gone.
So that’s what we do. We tell him to leave, making it obvious that we were kicking him out against his will. And then we detonate the IED. One of the ANA soldiers who had not taken cover caught a ball bearing but fortunately it was a ricochet and did nothing but bruise him.
We begin the slow slog back to our end of the road, making as random path as possible. We would even go through the middle of a Y-shaped tree instead of going around it. Choosing the most indirect route is always the safest way to travel, even if it is more difficult.

Some days later, when we were back at our end of the road, we were told what happened in that compound. The Taliban moved in after we had left. They didn't believe the old man's ruse and cut everyone's throats.

Everything here is depressing, I thought when I heard this. We force people out of their homes because we need the walls it to protect us at night. We try to kill people, because they are trying to kill us. There are bombs hidden where children play. Children are used as dickers. People are executed down the road beyond our reach. There are too many people to protect if we continue our advance, and there are too few of us to protect them. There are too many days to survive this place, and too many flies that never leave me alone. There will be too many questions if I get back. On the sat phone, I say nothing to anyone.

I don't know how to get back.

There's a hell of a contact going on down the road, but we didn't care. We lay in the corner of CP Bennet, everyone stripped to the waist and lying in the sun. It had been like this for a few days now. We had been taken off the road search for a reason I never found out, nor cared about. All that mattered each day was: were going out on the ground or not? If we were on QRF, it generally meant we would be left alone and safe behind high, thick mud walls.

I lay on my roll mat, wearing nothing but a pair of shorts and sunglasses, looking up at the brilliant blue sky, not seeing the bullets whizz about seven feet above me. All that bothered me were the incessant flies, making our bodies constantly twitch when they landed. They got so bad that the infantry sergeant-major had to come round with some bug repellent and smoked them out. This provided temporary relief, but they always came back.

We passed the time playing cards someone thought to bring. We did endless push-ups, cleaned weapons and did our dhobi. The Scouse showed us how to light a fire using a bow drill, from a survival course he had been on. And always, we tried to find out what we would be doing for the remaining time we had left on our tour. The new brigade was being deployed, while some of our brigade were starting to go home. No one wanted to get killed now. We heard horror stories of guys who had been killed within days of their end-date. Two were killed in Sangin by a car bomb in their final week.

Another, an American ATO had died on his last task by being complacent. More worryingly, we were informed that three Americans in the area had somehow been taken prisoner. Every now and again we would hear Taliban radio chatter about a prisoner being taken. When that happened, everyone must be accounted for. Every sergeant major of every squadron, company and battery walks around their lines, shining a torch at you to make sure you are there and not a prisoner. If you had been woken up by someone shining a torch in your face, you know the enemy have been bragging about a prisoner.

Some of the replacements had made their way to our little check point in the middle of I-still-have-no-idea-where. Pasty white skin and new combats. Most of them were eager and nervous looking. They asked the same questions we were asking six months ago, and we had long chats with them as we sat around the fire.

Two of them later had a close call. They were felling a tree with plastic explosives and either used too much or didn't take enough cover. The explosion shredded both their trousers and sent one back to Bastion hospital with leg injuries. It was the funniest thing we had heard of in a long time.

The evenings were spent lying in our doss bags, side by side, watching the first stars slowly appear in the sky with our rifles tucked into the bivvy bag for easy reach. As darkness grew, the stars came out in all their glory. I had forgotten what they truly looked like, remembering my African childhood.

Whoever got up first in the morning would relight the fire. On each side were two stone blocks and over it was an ammo tin of water. You put your breakfast rat-pack in the water and wait for the water to boil and enjoy a bit of peace and quiet before the world around you wake up.

One afternoon, I was on the sat phone to Anna. The fighting that day had been sporadic, but all we had to do was stay and help man the fort, taking turns at stag behind the gimpy in the tower. A claymore protected one flank, and the gun covered the other.

I had just come off stag and had stripped myself of helmet and body armour and was making the usual small talk with Anna, talking about life back home. I had begun to talk and think as if I would be part of that life again and was taking an interest in normal affairs.

An Apache had been flying overhead for a while, but we didn't usually take any notice of them anymore. Over the walls was a small field used as a helipad, and beyond that was another compound. This compound suddenly disappeared in an eruption of violence. I caught a glimpse of sparks shooting in all directions, dancing from left to right, and at the same time hundreds of deafening crackles. All this I saw in a fraction of a second before involuntarily ducking with my hands over my head, still holding the sat phone.
Another soldier had been politely waiting his turn and we both looked at each other.
"What the fuck was that?" someone asked in the following silence.
Over the walls, the neighbouring compound had disappeared in a giant cloud of brown dust. I had seen close support before, but I had never been so close. It was bloody loud and frightening. Only then did I realise that I was still on the phone to my fiancé. She had heard everything and when I put the receiver to my ear, I could hear her panicked voice saying a couple of times 'are you okay?'
"Yeah, I'm okay" I say, "everything is fine."
"You don't sound fine!"
"Nah, everything is fine. It was just a helicopter."
We found out later that the Apache had mistaken that compound for the enemy. Someone had made a mistake. I was just glad the mistake was that other compound and not ours.

9
Home

About a week remaining

Our turn at HRF finally arrives, when we had literally days left on tour. Helicopter Reaction Force was a much-coveted task. Unlike the other search teams out on the ground, the assigned team lived in the comfort and safety of Bastion, only getting flown out when needed in random parts of Helmand. As the Ginger Step Children of EOD, we had given up hope of getting our turn.

When we clambered out of the Chinook onto the flight line, we thought we were home free. We had just four days left online, and in those days, we did two tasks. Both IEDs had been found by infantry patrols who wanted them taken care of. So, we blew them up, spent the night in borrowed accommodation and in the morning waited for that reassuring *thwump thwump thwump* of the Chinook. It's a sound that I had come to love, and still love.

When the chopper drops us off, one of the first questions to be asked was 'when is it coming back to get us?' Like children being dropped off at a friend's house asking their mum when she was coming for them. And when it did come for us, we knew we were safe for the next few days.

Our last night of HRF, and our tour. We are going offline tomorrow. The team waited around at Bastion that day, enjoying the freedom but always aware of the time. If it gets to three o' clock, we definitely won't be going anywhere because of the lack of remaining daylight hours. By sunset, we knew we had made it.

That night, I am in one of the welfare portacabins, behind one of the computer screens lining the walls. I'm chatting on Facebook with Anna, and at last talking freely of near future plans. She wants to know what I'd like when I return. Do I want lots of people or to keep to myself? Do I know when the flight lands in the UK? When does my post tour leave start?

My answer is the same to everything. I don't know.

Everyone in the room stops typing briefly as a message is heard over the Bastion tannoy system. The speaker has to pause between words to prevent the echo taking over the entire message.

STANDBY-BY-BY... FOR BROADCAST-CAST-AST...THERE WILL BE-BE-BE-BE....A CONTROLLED DETONATION-TONATION-NATION............IN THIRTY SECONDS-CONDS....EVERYONE TAKE HARD COVER-OVER-ER...NOW-NOW-OW.
Everyone in the computer room continues with their social media time without any reaction whatsoever. I continue typing to Anna, vaguely interested in how large or how near the coming explosion would be. After a few seconds, a violent boom from outside is immediately followed by a large force that hits the cabins side on, as if a giant had thrown himself against the wall of the cabin. A few people laugh, but no one says a word. No one is interested.
"Don't worry babe, we're offline now. We're not going back out on the ground anymore."

We are woken up the next morning by someone from the ops room. He's come into our tent, with an alarmed look on his face.
"You lot are supposed to be on the flight line now" he is saying.
It took a while for us to respond, but we gradually sit upright in bed.
"We're offline mate" the Scouse says from the darkness.
"Sorry fellas, but they've brought you back online. You have a task."
Two days before our flight. We are livid and silent. No one says anything as we walk past the ops room, loaded with weapons, ammo, body armour, ECM, the ladder, batteries, medkits, more ammo, Vallon, Horn and Goldie.
They fly us out to Garmsir where we leave the safety of the FOB and tab to some location near a small canal. The IED is a fairly large one and shoots up its usual jet of earth into the sky, making a ring that floats off into the blue. We tab back to the FOB, not realising the kids who had been chatting with us had stolen my camera.

The Squadron Grown Ups have moved the remainder of our squadron into the large tent that had been used as the squadron gym. All the gym equipment has been shifted to one side and in its place are camp cots. The new squadron have moved into our tents. From there, they will leave their comfy kit and take the essentials out to wherever they will spend their tour. As for us, we live in the gym amongst mountains of bergans and daysacks of every size and description. There must have been thirty or forty of us crammed into that tent, and this time we were truly offline. For the first time in

months, we were reunited with the Gurkha teams we had trained with and spent an evening exchanging experiences. We told them about Gibbs, and they told us about Dave. Beaky had been shot in the side, but his body armour had saved him. He lifted his U-back and showed us the dressing they'd given him in the hospital. Luckily it was a glancing blow and merely spun him around. Another guy I had shared a room with in training had lost an arm and a leg. In total, the squadron had lost six killed and six severely wounded, not counting minor injuries like Beaky.
We had handed in all our ammo, our morphine, night vision goggles and search equipment, and suddenly we had nothing to do. I felt an immense relief to be alive and not to have to go out on the ground again and did not envy the new comers.
We had been told our danger money had been paid and we had all checked our bank accounts. It was about two thousand five hundred pounds in addition to our normal salary. After six months in Afghanistan, I had a little over ten thousand pounds.
I remember the first morning I woke up in that gym tent because of the nasty scare I had. I had been sleeping on my arm and cut off all the circulation so that when I woke up, it was completely numb. I had a couple of seconds of confusion and panic, not knowing where I was and not knowing why I could not move or feel my arm. The reason was obvious - I had been in an explosion and was lying on my side. My arm is gone. I felt the rising panic and sat up right in the camp cot, and feel my swinging arm hit my side. I look down at it, and then around. Everyone is still sleeping in the grey dawn light with the sound of soft snoring.
I lay back in my bed, relived and wondering if I had made any noise.

A couple of days later, we are loaded onto the flight out of the country. Forward of the entrance to the cabin is a seriously wounded soldier lying unconscious in a hospital bed, with an oxygen mask over his face. There's a nurse sitting next to him, keep watch as we all file past him to fill up from the back. He must have been wounded a few days before, so close to the end. They say that the bulk of casualties happen at the beginning or end of a tour, when soldiers are at first inexperienced and then become complacent.
On the flight, they serve us a couple of cans of Grolsch and fly us to Cyprus. At Camp Bloodhound, they put on a barbeque for us, and

provide some local expat comedian and musician. For ten hours, we sleep, shower, swim in the pool at one of the sovereign base areas and generally wait to continue the journey.
Bastion to Kabul. Kabul to Cyprus. Cyprus to Germany and finally we're flying over the fields of England. I stare down at the countryside below me as the plane comes in to land at Brize. Everything around us is so green.

The days after returning are a difficult. We were let out of camp the same day we arrived, as soon as our weapons were cleaned and handed into the armoury. Then each of our team went our separate ways to see our loved ones.
Anna met me at Waterloo, so did my brother. We left the station and walked around and they both noticed how jumpy I was. Someone closed their car door as we walked past them, and I involuntarily ducked.
I spent most of my post tour leave drinking and making wedding preparations, and when I wasn't doing that, I didn't know what to do with myself. I was sent a couple of times to Jordan for a few weeks to either help train other search teams or trial new search equipment, and being back in the military in the Middle East did a lot to keep my mind occupied. There were a lot of new faces in the squadron. Already they had sent more teams to replace us. One of them would be killed in their tour, but we didn't know that yet.

My first job after leaving the army was a labourer on a demolition site in London. For weeks I worked with Bulgarians, Romanians and Ukrainians for about eight pound an hour. The owner of the company was an ex-Royal Engineer and when he saw me coming to work in an old squadron t-shirt, he moved me to a better working site and upped my pay. I was working with two Ukrainians, a father and his son. When they found out that I had just left the army, the father told me in broken English that he had also been in the military.
"I was in Afghanistan" his son translated.
"I was in Afghanistan too" I said.
This old man looks me in the eye, takes my hand in both of his and says "my friend!"
I had joined the army to go to war. But what I discovered was the war films I had grown up watching don't tell the truth. Like so many

generations before me, I grew increasingly reluctant to talk about my war experiences which always came up once people knew I had been in the army. The question is always the same: 'were you in ever in a war?' It's almost always followed immediately with: 'did you ever kill anyone?'
I don't blame them. Those questions are almost certainly a product of a generation of gamers and endless streaming of war and action films with the same message: war is cool.
Eventually I avoided conversations, and then avoided people, not fitting in anywhere or even interested in trying.
The Ukrainian had done the same after he left, only feeling comfortable around other former soldiers. For us, we had left our lives and joined an institution that taught us how to kill people. They then sent us to a place neither of us had been to, to try to kill people we had never met and try not to let them kill us. We were even paid for it. And then suddenly, within two days we were back in normal life where it is not okay to kill people anymore. It isn't normal to sunbathe behind a wall with bullets flying over you, and be more annoyed about the flies than the bullets. You can't hear an explosion down the road and laugh at jokes about Taliban body parts. You definitely go through a doorway without checking for trip wires. You can't point a gun in someone's face and tell them to fuck off. I said that to a drunk Aussie outside Temple Walkabout who was being aggressive with my friend on a night out. I walked up to him and said "if you don't fuck off, I'm going to shoot you in your face." My new wife heard that. It scared her.
When you return to civvy street, you are well and truly on your own. To most people, Afghan was fought far away, with very little impact at home. They saw it on the news or heard the House of Whatever talking about it from time to time. But for those who returned, or the families of those who didn't return, it became a dominant feature in our lives.
Whenever I was alone in our new house, the background noises would fade away. I sit at the kitchen table and get tunnel vision until I am no longer in my kitchen. I'm up to my waist in water, with some others and everything is so real.
But I know I am in the UK.
The dark figure in front of me turns in the moonlight and helps me out of the irrigation canal and I can actually hear the noise of water

rushing off me as I climb out. He whispers in my ear, barely audible 'enemy ahead. Move left about five meters.'

My heartbeat is throbbing in my ears as I press the safety button and finger the trigger. I know Gibbs is there, and Dave. We kneel in herringbone formation, waiting for the shooting to start, and wait and wait until the morning bin lorries wake me up.